Jayne Netley Mayhew's

Cross Stitch
JUNGLE

20 breath-taking designs

D&C
David and Charles

www.mycraftivity.com

David & Charles is an F+W Publications Inc. company
4700 East Galbraith Road, Cincinnati, OH 45236

First published in the UK and US in 2008

Text, designs and illustrations copyright © Jayne Netley Mayhew 2008
Layout and photography copyright © David & Charles 2008

For Ian, and my friend Wendy

ISBN-13: 978-0-7153-2644-2 hardback
ISBN-10: 0-7153-2644-9 hardback

Printed in China by SNP Leefung
for David & Charles
Brunel House   Newton Abbot   Devon

Senior Commissioning Editor: Cheryl Brown
Desk Editor: Bethany Dymond
Project Editor: Lin Clements
Art Editor: Charly Bailey
Photographer: Kim Sayer and Karl Adamson
Production Controller: Ros Napper

Visit our website at www.davidandcharles.co.uk

David & Charles books are available from all good bookshops; alternatively you can contact our Orderline on 0870 9908222 or write to us at FREEPOST EX2 110, D&C Direct, Newton Abbot, TQ12 4ZZ (no stamp required UK only); US customers call 800-289-0963 and Canadian customers call 800-840-5220.

CONTENTS

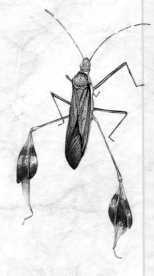

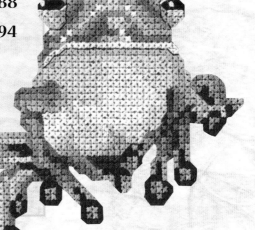

INTO THE JUNGLE. . .

In this book I bring you a selection of beautiful designs from a truly amazing part of our world – the jungles of the tropical rainforest. These extraordinary regions are an essential part of our planet's ecosystem, and so are vital for our survival too. The biological riches of these vast tracts of land are breathtaking in their beauty, colour, shape and size. And yet even today there are areas that remain a mystery to us, with flora and fauna still waiting to be discovered.

The cross stitch designs are a mixture of some of the best-known animals, birds, reptiles and insects from Asia to the Amazon, from the tops of lofty trees down to the tangled jungle floor. We begin with an impressive portrait of a snarling tiger, dramatically placed on a black background. There is also a beautifully dappled jaguar swimming along a creek bed and a charming study of an ocelot.

Large animals such as the elephant and rhinoceros have been included, and Asian elephants are shown working with their Indian mahouts. A lone rhino emerges from the forest into a sunlit glade, reminding us what a truly impressive animal he is. For sheer oddity the sloth is hard to beat – many of us might like a life in slow motion, for a while anyway. Tapirs have remained virtually unchanged for 35 million years and two young tapirs have lost none of their charm. Amid the leafy boughs of the dense jungle canopy we have a charming pair of squirrel monkeys and also a devoted orang-utan mother and her sweet baby.

A whole book could be devoted to the glory of jungle birds, birds so rich in colour that the designs sing out from the page. There are stunning scarlet and hyacinth macaws, a toucan with his amazing beak waiting to feast on juicy

fruit, a fabulous bird of paradise in a shimmer of feathers as he displays for his mate and a truly exquisite peacock.

Jungle regions are home to some remarkable and unusual creatures, such as a large boa constrictor, curled around a fern-covered bower. There is also the chameleon, an extraordinary colour impersonator, and the scaly magnificence of the prehistoric-looking iguana. There are many thousands of smaller jungle inhabitants, such as breathtakingly beautiful butterflies and vividly coloured tree frogs – too many for individual portraits so I have brought you a glorious mass of them in two contemporary designs.

Lastly, I have included a snapshot of the human inhabitants of this tropical world, the Kayapo Indians, dancing for their forest spirits. Even today we are still discovering more about the fascinating Indian tribes of the vast Amazon region, and are realizing, sadly, that many of these have disappeared, and along with them their culture and knowledge.

So, I bring you a slice of vibrant jungle life – from the teeming leaf litter to the dense jungle canopy. I hope that my selection of designs will soon have you reaching eagerly for needle and thread for many hours of enjoyable stitching.

Jayne Netley Mayhew

JUNGLE INSPIRATIONS

This section gives you some ideas on how you can use the fabulous designs in this book to create smaller projects, ideal for when time is short, but still bringing that lush jungle feel to your home. Smaller areas of the main designs can be selected and used for a wide range of attractive items (see here and overleaf). The finished sizes of these smaller projects can be altered depending on the fabric count you use. For a larger finished design, work on a fabric with a lower count, such as 12-count or 11-count. For a smaller finished size, work on a finer fabric, perhaps 16- or 18-count. Use three strands of thread for 12-count, two for 16-count and one for 18-count.

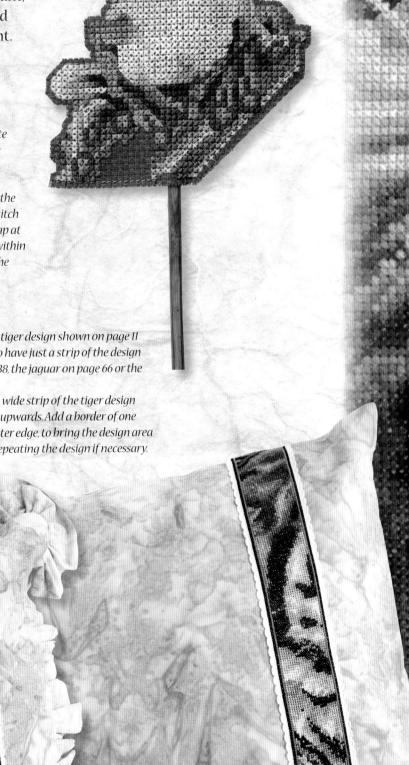

FROG PLANT STICK

Individual frogs can be taken from the design on page 35 to create smaller projects, such as this fun plant stick. You could also make a plant stick using the butterflies charted on pages 74–75.

Work the frog on a 12.7cm (5in) square of Christmas green 14-count Aida (DMC code 500) from the chart on page 36/37. Place the embroidery over a square of complementary coloured felt and stitch together closely around the edge of the design, leaving a small gap at the base for the plant stick to be pushed into. Trim the fabric to within a stitch width all around the design, taking care not to cut into the design area. Insert the stick to finish.

TIGER STRIPE CUSHIONS

These cushions only need the additional of a narrow strip of the tiger design shown on page 11 to create some stylish home accessories. Other designs could also have just a strip of the design worked, perhaps for towels or bed linen – try the ocelot on page 38, the jaguar on page 66 or the peacock on page 88.

Stitch on 5cm (2in) wide 26-stitch Aida band. Take a 22-stitch wide strip of the tiger design charted on pages 12–15, and work from the bottom of the design upwards. Add a border of one row of rust (DMC 3826) and one row of black (DMC 310) to each outer edge, to bring the design area up to 26 stitches wide. Stitch until you reach the desired length, repeating the design if necessary. See page 103 for making up a frilled cushion.

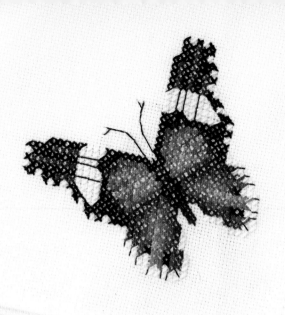

BUTTERFLY NAPKINS

Individual butterflies can be taken from the design on page 73 to create a range of smaller projects, such as these napkins. You could also mount them into coasters, key rings, fridge magnets and many other ready-made items.

Work on a 33cm (13in) square of white 22-count evenweave. Turn and hem the edge of the napkin before stitching the butterflies. Work the butterfly from the chart on page 74, first over two fabric threads about 2.5cm (1in) from the corner of the napkin and then over just one thread in the other corner, to create a smaller butterfly.

By working on different fabric counts the finished size of the design can be changed, making it smaller or larger – see page 99 for Changing Design Sizes.

ORANG-UTAN PICTURE

The baby orang-utan from page 48 makes the sweetest picture and would be quicker to stitch than the full design.

Work the baby from the chart on pages 50–53 on a 28 x 33cm (11 x 13in) piece of white 16-count Aida. I used an 87 x 112 stitch count area of the design of the baby. The top edge of the design area is one stitch away from the top of the baby's head and one stitch away from the edge of his left arm. The finished design size is 12.7 x 17.8cm (5 x 7in). Follow the stitching instructions for the main design on page 48.

JUNGLE CAMEOS

Here are some more ideas for using the designs in the book for quick-stitch projects. The larger designs can be cropped to produce some interesting little portraits, as shown here. Remember too, that you can stitch the designs on different fabric colours, which will also create a different look.

Find some individual frogs from the chart on pages 36–37 and stitch them for stuffed toys or cards. If making a child's toy, stitch on to a larger count, perhaps 12-count using three strands of thread. Back with felt and stuff with some polyester filling.

A charming cameo picture of a squirrel monkey is easily created. Work just a single monkey from the chart on page 22/23, omitting any stitches from the right-hand edge of the design.

Working just the beautiful head of the peacock from page 91 would make a lovely bookmark or greetings card.

A hyacinth macaw can be worked as a small cameo by using part of the design from page 18. Working one long piece of the design would make a wonderful bell pull. Just the head and body could be worked on a smaller fabric count, perhaps 16- or 18-count to create a smaller design for a lovely card.

TIGER

Of all the jungle animals the tiger is perhaps the best known and the most instantly recognisable. Native to eastern and southern Asia, with the largest population in India, the tiger is the largest of the big cats and one of the top predators in the animal kingdom. It is certainly one of the most magnificent, a true king of the beasts. The beautifully marked coat has a distinctive pattern of dark vertical stripes over red-orange fur, allowing the tiger to disappear into the shadows of vegetation.

Sadly, fur poaching and destruction of habitat have greatly reduced the numbers of wild tigers and all species are now endangered. Conservation efforts continue. Long in tooth and strong in claw, long may tigers reign over the jungle floors.

Tooth and Claw

Stitch count 220h x 245w
Design size 40 x 44.5cm (15¾ x 17½in)

YOU WILL NEED

❋ 56 x 61cm (22 x 24in) black 14-count Aida
❋ DMC stranded cotton (floss) as listed in the chart key
  (1 skein of each colour but 2 skeins of 310, 975, 938, 647, 3826)
❋ Tapestry needle size 24–26
❋ Suitable picture frame

1 Prepare your fabric and mark the centre point (see page 99). Work outwards from the centre of the fabric and the centre of the chart on pages 12–15.

2 Work over one Aida block, using two strands of stranded cotton (floss) for cross stitch. Only whole cross stitches are used in this design.

3 Once all the stitching is complete, check for missed stitches, remove any guidelines and then mount and frame the picture (see page 102 for advice).

The tiger's great bulk and power make it an awesome predator. They can grow to 4m (13ft) in length and can weigh up to 300kg (660lbs). Despite this they can reach speeds of 50—65 km/h (35—40mph) and can jump as high as 5m (16ft).

This dramatic,
snarling tiger is
shown stitched on
black Aida for maximum
impact but would look equally
impressive if stitched on
a sage green or khaki
coloured fabric.

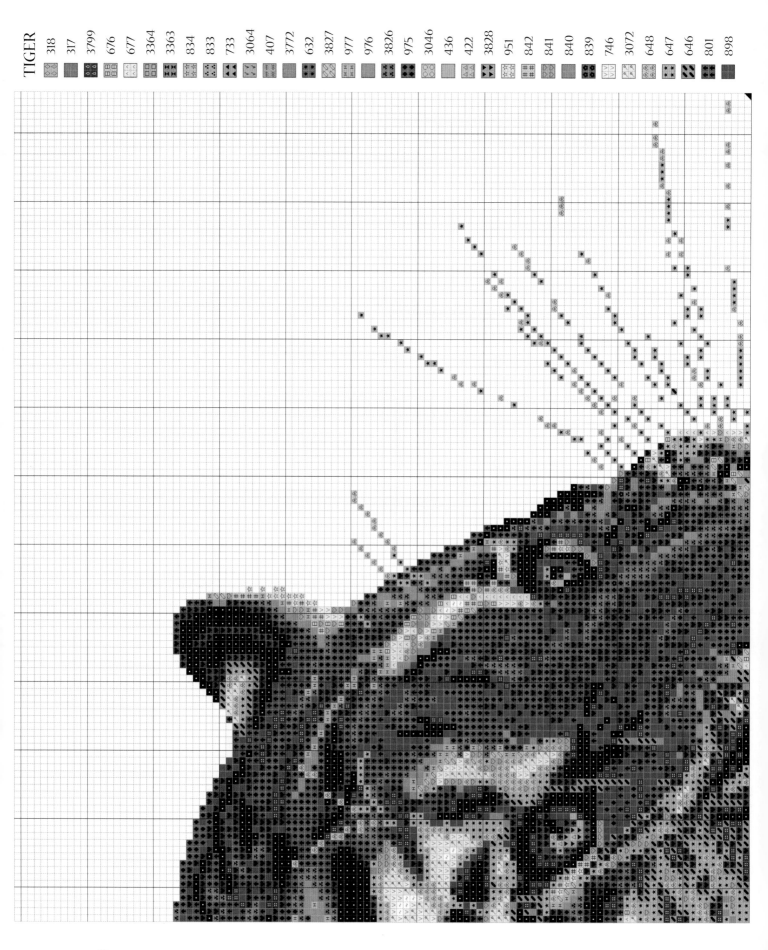

938 3371 White 310

Tiger 13

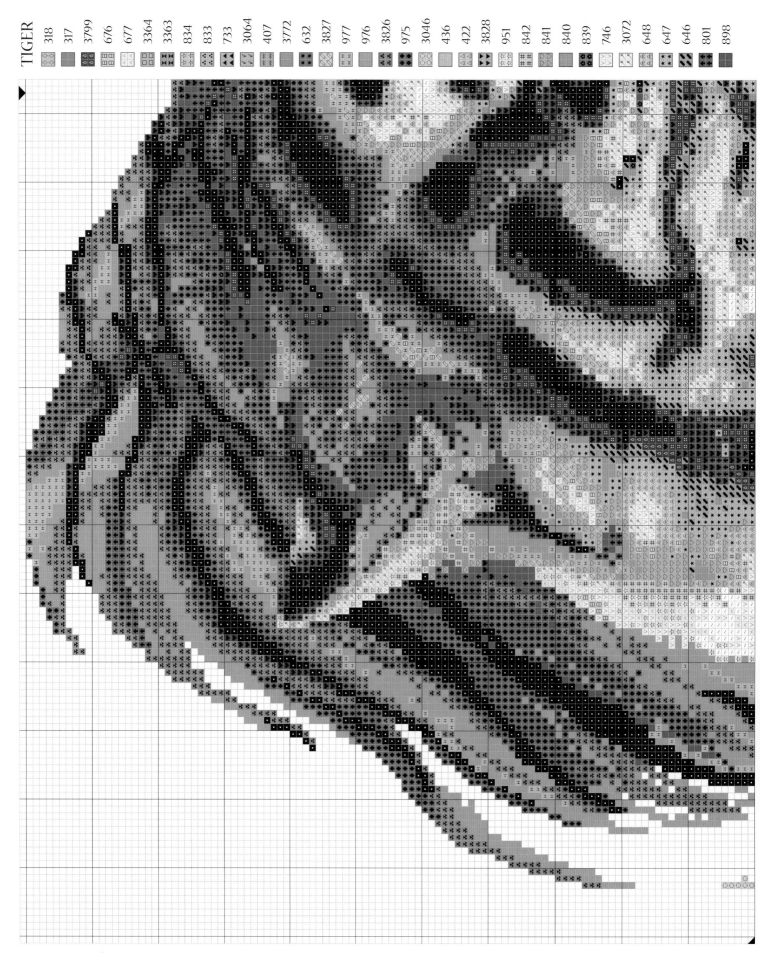

TIGER

318 317 3799 676 677 3364 3363 834 833 733 3064 407 3772 632 3827 977 976 3826 975 3046 436 422 3828 951 842 841 840 839 746 3072 648 647 646 801 898

14 Tiger

Tiger 15

HYACINTH MACAW

These fabulous birds are members of the parrot family and are native to the forests of central South America. The superb colouring of cobalt blue and contrasting yellow face markings makes the hyacinth macaw a very distinctive bird. They are the largest flying parrot, measuring 1m (3ft) from head to tip of the tail, with a wing span of over a metre.

The hyacinth macaw is a very sociable bird and is usually found in flocks of a dozen or more. A pair of birds will bond for life and rear one chick a year, nesting in holes almost exclusively in manduvi trees, which themselves are rather rare. Fledglings stay with their parents for 6–18 months, forming a highly sociable family group.

Heavenly Blues

Stitch count 200h x 100w
Design size 36.3 x 18.2cm (14¼ x 7¼in)

YOU WILL NEED

※ 53.5 x 35.5cm (21 x 14in) sky blue 28-count linen (DMC code 762)
※ DMC stranded cotton (floss) as listed in the chart key (1 skein of each colour)
※ Tapestry needle size 24–26
※ Suitable picture frame

1 Prepare your fabric and mark the centre point (see page 99). Work outwards from the centre of the fabric and the centre of the chart overleaf.

2 Work over two threads of linen, using two strands of stranded cotton (floss) for full and three-quarter cross stitches. Work the backstitch with one strand of black for the eye detail. For the eye highlights work a French knot with one strand of white.

3 Once all the stitching is complete, check for missed stitches, remove any guidelines and then mount and frame the picture (see page 102 for advice).

Hyacinth macaws have the strongest beaks of all birds, allowing them to feast on their favourite foods and crack very hard nuts and seeds — even coconuts and macadamia nuts. They also eat various fruits and other vegetable matter.

Eleven different shades of blue have been used in this design to achieve the richness of colour and depth of tone for the birds' plumage, ranging from dark indigo to pale sky blue.

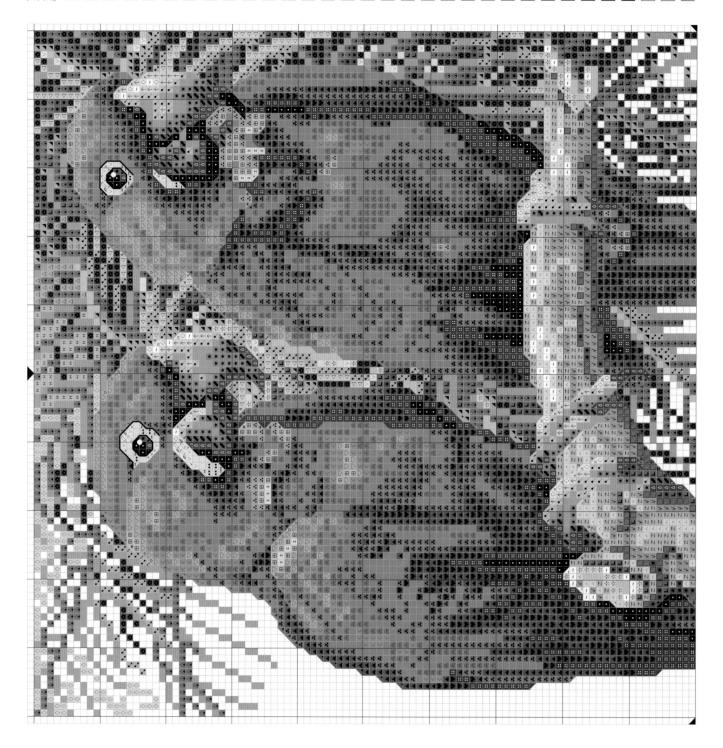

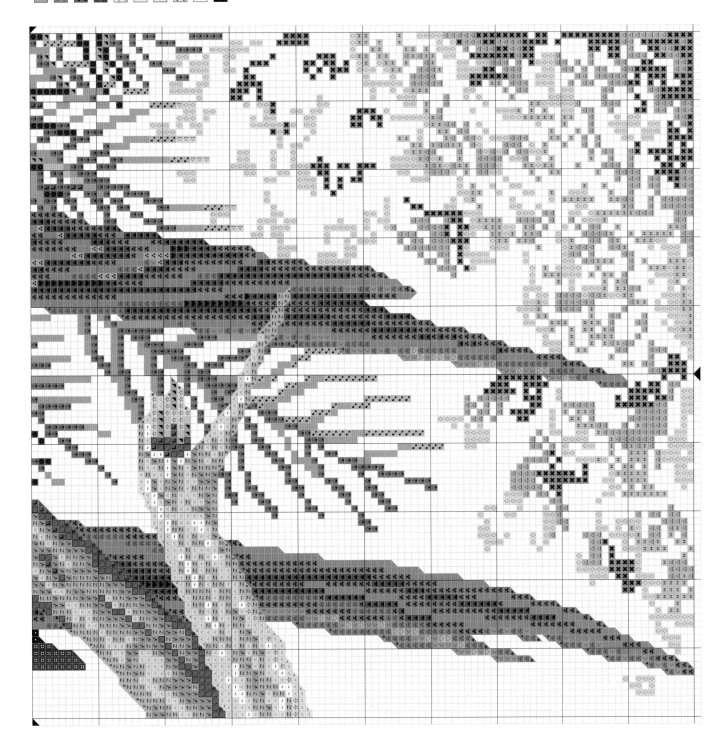

414 317 413 3799 3078 445 307 444 White 310

SQUIRREL MONKEY

These cute and nimble monkeys live in troops of about 40 to 50 members, although these groups can reach 200 or more. They can be found in the tropical rainforests of Central and South America – from Costa Rica through central Brazil and Bolivia.

They are perfectly adapted to the rainforest environment, being agile, sharp-eyed and with excellent co-ordination. Moving freely between the ground and the highest branches of the canopy with ease, they forage for fruits, seeds, flowers and leaves. They often follow along behind other monkeys picking off insects that have been disturbed. Their tails are longer than their whole body length and although they cannot grasp with it, as some monkeys can, it is essential for balance as they leap among the trees.

Sweet and Nimble

Stitch count 200h x 100w
Design size 36.3 x 18.2cm (14¼ x 7¼in)

YOU WILL NEED

※ 53.5 x 35.5cm (21 x 14in) blue 14-count Aida (DMC code 3840)
※ DMC stranded cotton (floss) as listed in the chart key (1 skein of each colour)
※ Tapestry needle size 24–26
※ Suitable picture frame

1 Prepare your fabric and mark the centre point (see page 99). Work outwards from the centre of the fabric and the centre of the chart overleaf.

2 Work over two threads of linen, using two strands of stranded cotton (floss) for cross stitch. Work the backstitch with one strand of black around the eye. Work French knots with one strand of white for the eye highlights.

3 Once all the stitching is complete, check for missed stitches, remove any guidelines and then mount and frame the picture (see page 102 for advice).

Although squirrel monkeys are small in stature they have a large brain in proportion to their body and have the largest brain mass to body mass ratio of all the primates — about 1:17. The human ratio is 1:35.

These squirrel monkeys are shown perched at the top of the tree canopy ready to set off in search of fruit and insects. They remain alert though to the aerial threat of large falcons.

3047	3046	3045	167	613	612	611	610	165	166	3013	3012	3011	833	831	934	472	471	470	469	936	356	3778	758

754	948	976	977	3827	3855	3823	677	422	3828	420	869	801	938	3371	762	415	318	414	317	413	3799	White	310

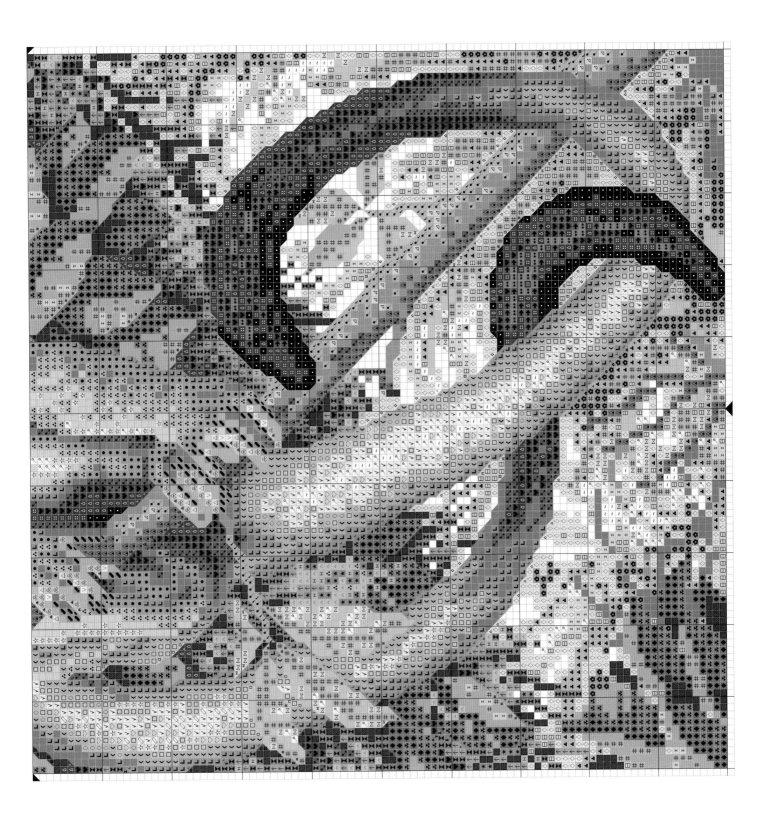

IGUANA

Iguanas are truly fascinating creatures. They are lizards native to tropical areas of central and South America and the Caribbean. The Green Iguana shown here can be found over a wide and varied geographical area, from Mexico to Paraguay and also in Texas, Florida and Hawaii.

Iguanas have spines along their back to protect them from predators and a dewlap hanging beneath their head to help regulate body temperature. They possess sharp teeth to allow them to shred and digest vegetation and have excellent eyesight, which enables them to see over long distance as well as discerning shapes, colour, shadows and movement.

Prehistoric Link

Stitch count 150h x 100w
Design size 27.3 x 18.2cm (10¾ x 7¼in)

YOU WILL NEED

※ 43.2 x 35.5cm (17 x 14in) sky blue 14-count Aida (DMC code 800)
※ DMC stranded cotton (floss) as listed in the chart key (1 skein of each colour)
※ Tapestry needle size 24–26
※ Suitable picture frame

1 Prepare your fabric and mark the centre point (see page 99). Work outwards from the centre of the fabric and the centre of the chart overleaf.

2 Work over one block of Aida, using two strands of stranded cotton (floss) for full and three-quarter cross stitches.

3 Work the backstitch with one strand of 310 for the butterfly, the iguana's eye and body detail. Use one strand of 452 for the eye detail, 3031 and 3862 for the body detail. Note: for clarity the backstitch colours on the chart are shown as follows: red = 310, blue = 3031, green = 3862. Work a French knot with one strand of white for the eye highlights and one strand of 977 for the ends of the butterfly antennae.

4 Once all the stitching is complete, check for missed stitches, remove any guidelines and then mount and frame the picture (see page 102 for advice).

Iguanas use their keen eyesight to find their way through dense forest vegetation as well as for finding food. Visual signals, such as head bobbing, are also used to communicate with other iguanas.

The scales that cover a lizard are made of a substance called keratin, which is also the basis of human hair. This design makes use of a lot of backstitch detail to define the scales and the facial features.

IGUANA

3862	779	453
3031	543	452
White	3864	3861
310	3863	3860

801	977	987	3011
938	976	986	164
762	3826	936	989
415	975	934	988

			Backstitch:
3363	830	869	red = 310
3362	832	420	blue = 3031
3013	834	3828	green = 3862
3012	3364	422	

Iguana 27

ELEPHANT

Asian elephants have been tamed and worked by humans for more than 4,000 years and are found in India, Bangladesh, Sri Lanka, Indochina and Indonesia. Even though they are huge, elephants move easily through mud and marshes and are more adept than horses in mountainous terrain, moving people, stone, wood and other goods. Within the Asian culture and religion they have been worshipped and revered for centuries, and are still used for ceremonial purposes today.

Working elephants are cared for and worked by keepers called mahouts. A master mahout teaches a young man, usually his son, passing on his knowledge. It takes around 20 years to train a master mahout and an elephant can live for 60 years, so for a mahout it is a lifelong bond.

Gentle Working Giants

Stitch count 210h x 180w
Design size 38 x 33cm (15 x 13in)

YOU WILL NEED

※ 53.5 x 48.5cm (21 x 19in) sand 28-count linen (DMC code 739)
※ DMC stranded cotton (floss) as listed in the chart key
  (1 skein of each colour but 2 skeins of 642 and 640)
※ Tapestry needle size 24–26
※ Suitable picture frame

1 Prepare your fabric and mark the centre point (see page 99). Work outwards from the centre of the fabric and the centre of the chart on pages 30–33.

2 Work over two threads of linen, using two strands of stranded cotton (floss) for full and three-quarter cross stitches.

3 Once all the stitching is complete, check for missed stitches, remove any guidelines and then mount and frame the picture (see page 102 for advice).

The Asian elephant has been used in forestry for centuries and my design shows two elephants being used to move large logs, which they do easily using their tusks and trunk.

ELEPHANT

⊞	372
▷	371
○	370
▨	936
▪	934
◿	3013
⊞	3012
▲	3011
L	318
▨	414
▨	413
I	613
V	612
⊞	611
◆	610
⊠	677
□	422
⋰	3828
▨	420
◀	869
◿	3033
Ƨ	3782
⋰	3032
▲	3790
△	822
⋰	644
★	642
▨	640
♥	3787
▦	3021
V	950
▨	3064
⊞	3772
▨	632

▨	300	♥	334
◢	801	▨	312
▨	938	I	336
H	3371	U	3348
⋮	White	░	3053
●	310	I	3052

Elephant 31

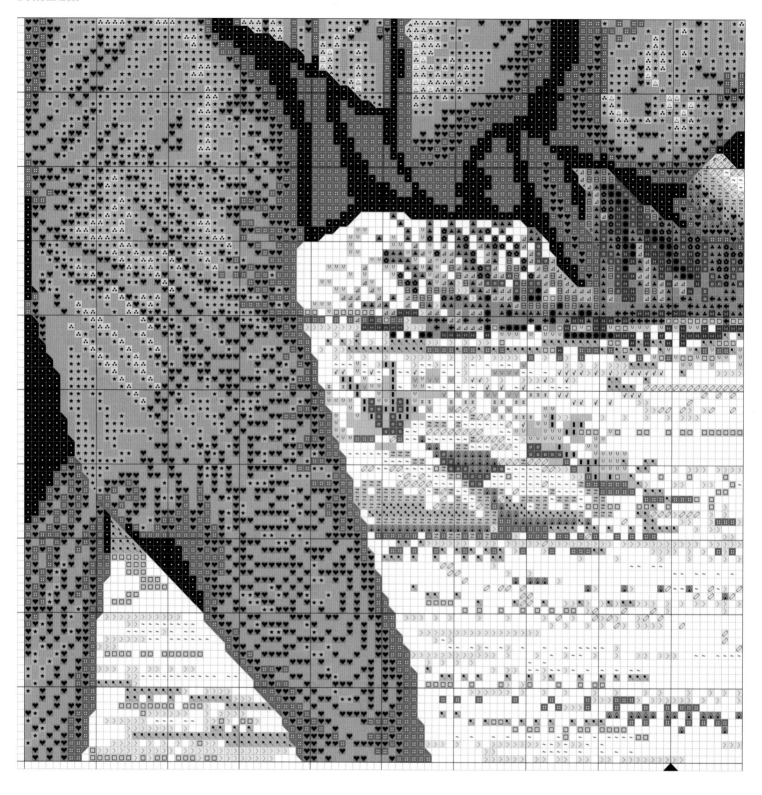

ELEPHANT

⊞	372
▷	371
◦◦	370
▦	936
◦◦	934
⊿	3013
⊞	3012
▲▲	3011
ʟʟ	318
▦	414
▦	413
ɪɪ	613
ᴠᴠ	612
▦	611
◆◆	610
⁖	677
▱	422
◆	3828
▦	420
◆◆	869
◿◿	3033
ᴢᴢ	3782
⁘	3032
▲▲	3790
△△	822
⁙	644
★★	642
▦	640
♥♥	3787
⁙	3021
ᴠᴠ	950
◦◦	3064
⌗⌗	3772
▦	632

▓	300	▨	334
◪	801	▦	312
▦	938	⌗⌗	336
ʜʜ	3371	ᴜᴜ	3348
⌐	White	▦	3053
▪	310	▌⌗	3052

TREE FROGS

Frogs can be found all over the world, from sub-artic to tropical regions, although most are found in tropical rainforests. The jungle frogs shown here, often called tree frogs, come in all shapes and sizes. Some of these amphibians are vividly coloured – bright yellow, green or red; others are so well camouflaged you would not see them unless they moved. Some are as small as your little fingernail, while others are as big as a dinner plate.

Generally, these frogs live on the ground and in trees, laying their eggs somewhere moist – in pools or in water that has collected in a nook or leaf in the trees. The tadpoles need to be washed by the rain down into the pools. They mostly feed on insects and other invertebrates.

Forest Gems

Stitch count 110h x 150w
Design size 20 x 27.3cm (7¾ x 10¾in)

YOU WILL NEED

❋ 35.5 x 43cm (14 x 17in) black 14-count Aida
❋ DMC stranded cotton (floss) as listed in the chart key
　(1 skein of each colour but 2 skeins of 310)
❋ Tapestry needle size 24–26
❋ Suitable picture frame

1 Prepare your fabric and mark the centre point (see page 99). Work outwards from the centre of the fabric and the centre of the chart overleaf.

2 Work over one block of Aida, using two strands of stranded cotton (floss) for full and three-quarter cross stitches. Work the backstitch with one strand of black or white for the eye and mouth details. For the eye highlights work a French knot with one strand of white.

3 Once all the stitching is complete, check for missed stitches, remove any guidelines and then mount and frame the picture (see page 102 for advice).

Amid the blaze of colour in this design there are 24 frogs. You could stitch the whole design for a contemporary picture or cushion, or stitch individual frogs for smaller projects (see page 7).

The vivid colouring of some frogs is often a sign that they are toxic, but not always. These toxins make the frog distasteful to predators but can be powerful enough to cause paralysis and even death. Some South American natives use the toxin from the poison dart frog when hunting.

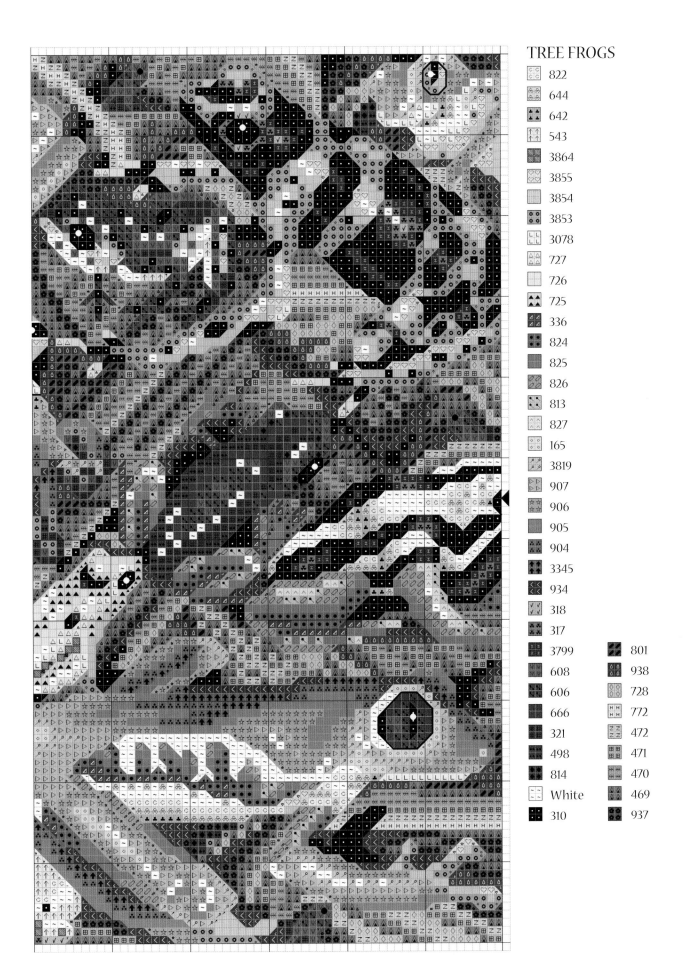

TREE FROGS

Symbol	Color
C C C	822
	644
	642
↑ ↑	543
	3864
♥ ♥	3855
	3854
◊ ◊	3853
L L L	3078
△ △	727
	726
▲ ▲	725
	336
	824
	825
	826
	813
∧ ∧	827
◊ ◊	165
	3819
▷ ▷	907
☆ ☆	906
	905
	904
↟ ↟	3345
< <	934
∨ ∨	318
	317
	3799
	608
	606
	666
	321
	498
	814
- -	White
	310

Symbol	Color
	801
	938
	728
H H	772
Z Z	472
⊞ ⊞	471
	470
▲ ▲	469
	937

OCELOT

Rosettes, spots and stripes on a tawny background make this beautiful wild cat highly distinctive and in the past, hundreds of thousands of ocelots were killed for their fur. It is the largest of the small cats of the rainforest and can be found all over South and Central America and Mexico.

The ocelot is one of the top predators: it is mostly nocturnal, solitary and has extremely flexible joints, which enable it to swim well and climb trees with ease. Using the jungle vegetation as cover, the dark spots and stripes break up the cat's outline amid the shadows, making them very successful hunters. It has an excellent sense of smell and good night vision. Their prey is mostly small creatures, including monkeys, birds, snakes, fish and rodents.

Nocturnal Perfection

Stitch count 150h x 110w
Design size 27.3 x 20cm (10¾ x 7¾in)

YOU WILL NEED

❊ 43 x 35.5cm (17 x 14in) light green 28-count linen (DMC code 772)
❊ DMC stranded cotton (floss) as listed in the chart key (1 skein of each colour)
❊ Tapestry needle size 24–26
❊ Suitable picture frame

1 Prepare your fabric and mark the centre point (see page 99). Work outwards from the centre of the fabric and the centre of the chart overleaf.

2 Work over two threads of linen, using two strands of stranded cotton (floss) for the cross stitches. Only whole cross stitches are used in this design.

3 Once all the stitching is complete, check for missed stitches, remove any guidelines and then mount and frame the picture (see page 102 for advice).

Ocelots rest in dense foliage or in trees during the day. Like other small cats, they sit with their tails curled around their bodies, whereas large cats like the leopard normally sit with their tails extended out behind them.

This design emphasizes the ocelot's gloriously spotted and striped coat. The fur resembles that of a jaguar and it is sometimes called the painted jaguar.

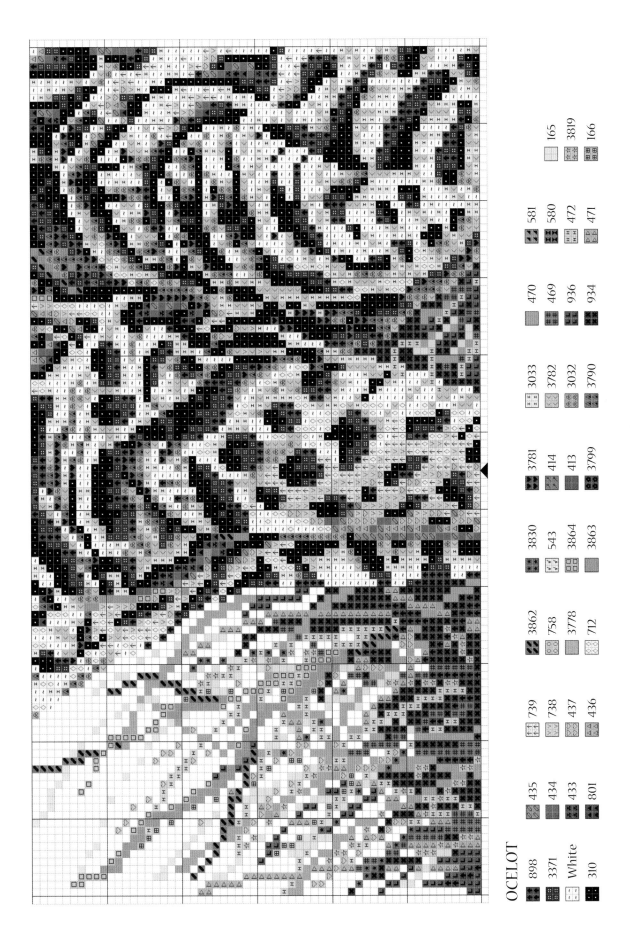

OCELOT

898	435	739	3862	3830
3371	434	738	758	543
White	433	437	3778	3864
310	801	436	712	3863

3781	3033	581	165
414	3782	580	3819
413	3032	472	166
3799	3790	471

470
469
936
934

TOUCAN

The toucan is a colourful bird found over a wide geographical area from Mexico to Argentina. The toucan's most distinctive feature is its bill, which though large and spectacular, is actually quite light as it is supported internally with thin rods of bone and filled with air cells. The Toco toucan is the largest of all the toucan species, with a huge 19cm (7½in) long bill.

Toucans are sociable birds and live in small communities of several families. They use holes in tree trunks in much the same way that woodpeckers do. While they are mainly fruit eaters, they will also eat nuts, insects and even small lizards and bats. The food is moved from the tip of the bill to the mouth with a quick backward toss of the head.

Fruit Fits the Bill

Stitch count 110h x 90w
Design size 20 x 16.5cm (7¾ x 6½in)

YOU WILL NEED

※ 35.5 x 33cm (14 x 13in) sky blue 14-count Aida (DMC code 800)
※ DMC stranded cotton (floss) as listed in the chart key (1 skein of each colour)
※ Tapestry needle size 24–26
※ Suitable picture frame

1 Prepare your fabric and mark the centre point (see page 99). Work outwards from the centre of the fabric and the centre of the chart overleaf.

2 Work over one block of Aida, using two strands of stranded cotton (floss) for full and three-quarter cross stitches. Work the backstitch with one strand of black for the eye detail and one strand of 3787 for the ant detail.

3 Once all the stitching is complete, check for missed stitches, remove any guidelines and then mount and frame the picture (see page 102 for advice).

Toucans are one of the noisiest birds in the jungle. From high up in the trees they call out to each other – not a sweet, trilling birdsong, but a deep, snoring croak, which can be heard for up to 0.8km (½ a mile).

This design shows the toucan amid his favourite food – fruit of any kind. That amazing bill is all the more distinctive when contrasted with the glossy black plumage.

TOUCAN

946	742	413	796	640	823	937	3787
900	741	3799	318	3843	822	469	3021
White	740	744	414	995	644	470	934	3823
310	947	743	317	797	642	336	935	745

44 Toucan

TAPIR

3046 3045 167 3053 3052 3051 782 613 612 611 3013 3012 3011 472 471 470 469 937 934 543 842 841 840 712 739 738 437 436 435 434 433 801 938 3371 White 310

Tapir 45

TAPIR

Tapirs are large pig-like animals with short, prehensile snouts. There are four species, all of which are classified as endangered, and they can be found in jungle regions of South and Central America and Southeast Asia.

Tapirs do not stray far from water, where they can make an amphibious escape from a predator at a moment's notice. Water also allows them to cool off during the hottest parts of the day. Brazilian and Baird's tapirs have thick skin on the back of the neck and a short, bristly mane, which provides some protection from jaguar bites. Short, slender legs and a stocky body enable them to push through dense undergrowth to forage for tender shoots, fruits and berries with their mobile and sensitive snout.

The Sweetest Babies

Stitch count 90h x 110w
Design size 16.5 x 20cm (6½ x 7¾in)

YOU WILL NEED

❉ 33 x 35.5cm (13 x 14in) cream 14-count Aida
❉ DMC stranded cotton (floss) as listed in the chart key
 (1 skein of each colour)
❉ Tapestry needle size 24–26
❉ Suitable picture frame

1 Prepare your fabric and mark the centre point (see page 99). Work outwards from the centre of the fabric and the centre of the chart on page 45.

2 Work over one block of Aida, using two strands of stranded cotton (floss) for the cross stitches. Only whole cross stitches are used in the design.

3 Once all the stitching is complete, check for missed stitches, remove any guidelines and then mount and frame the picture (see page 102 for advice).

Tapirs have been known to sink to the bottom of a water source, submerging themselves completely and walking along the river bed in order that small fish can pick parasites off their skin.

Spots and stripes help camouflage baby tapirs in dappled forest light. Hunting young tapirs is risky for a predator, as on hearing a squeal from her baby the mother comes running, like an express battering ram, jaws snapping.

ORANG-UTAN

The name orang-utan derives from the Malay word *orang* which means 'person' and *hutan* which means 'forest' – thus 'person of the forest'. Gentle and enigmatic, their liquid brown eyes shine with intelligence. With a blazing crown of reddish-orange fur, glowing as if touched by the sun, they are the very essence of the jungle forest. They spend most of their time in the trees, sleeping in nests made from branches and leaves. They predominantly eat fruit, but will also eat young shoots and leaves, seeds, insects and birds' eggs.

Orang-utans are currently only found in the rainforests of Borneo and Sumatra, though originally were more widely distributed. The Bornean species is classified as highly endangered and the Sumatran species is now critically endangered, for the usual reason – destruction of their habitat by humans.

Devoted Mother

Stitch count 220h x 220w
Design size 40 x 40cm (15¾ x 15¾in)

YOU WILL NEED

※ 56 x 56cm (22 x 22in) blue 14-count Aida (DMC code 3747)
※ DMC stranded cotton (floss) as listed in the chart key (1 skein of each colour but 2 skeins of 301, 3826, 938, 898 and 976 and 3 skeins of 801, 400 and 300)
※ Tapestry needle size 24–26
※ Suitable picture frame

1 Prepare your fabric and mark the centre point (see page 99). Work outwards from the centre of the fabric and the centre of the chart on pages 50–53.

2 Work over one Aida block, using two strands of stranded cotton (floss) for full and three-quarter cross stitches. Work the backstitch with two strands of black for the baby's upper eye detail and 938 for the lower eye detail. Use black for the mother's backstitch eye detail and 3371 for her mouth detail. Use 469 for the backstitch on the leaf stems.

3 Once all the stitching is complete, check for missed stitches, remove any guidelines and then mount and frame the picture (see page 102 for advice).

Orang-utans are very intelligent (their genetic make–up is 97% the same as ours) and they regularly use tools. Like us, they don't much like sitting in the rain, and will use leaves not only to make rain hats but also as leak–proof roofs over their sleeping nests.

This touching design shows the relationship between mother and baby orang-utan. They are constant companions, inseparable for the first eight years of the youngster's life.

ORANG-UTAN

898	975	676	3864	642	470	733	832
938	301	3827	3863	640	469	732	831
3371	400	977	3862	3787	937	730	830
White	300	976	746	3021	934	472	829	834
310	801	3826	677	543	644	471	734	833

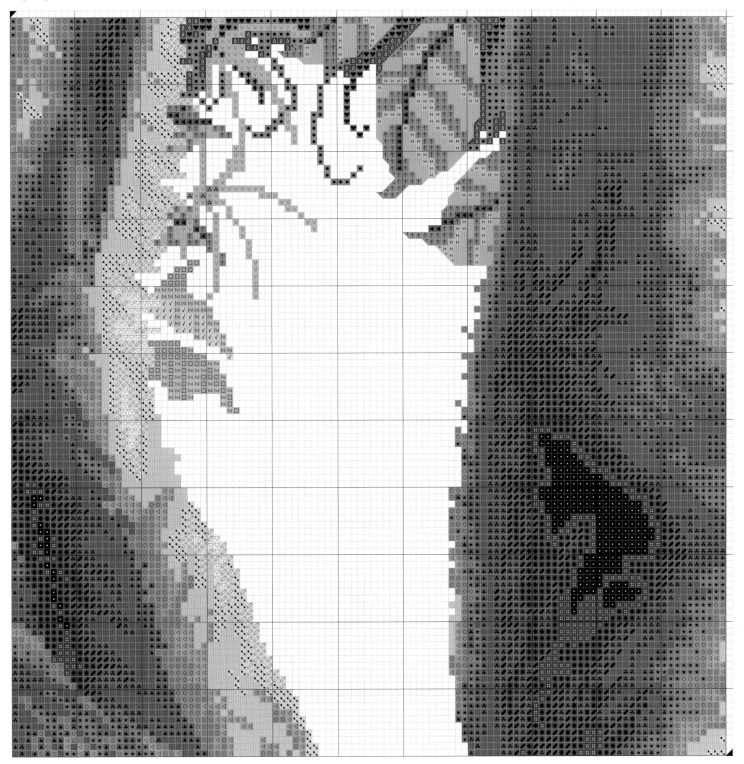

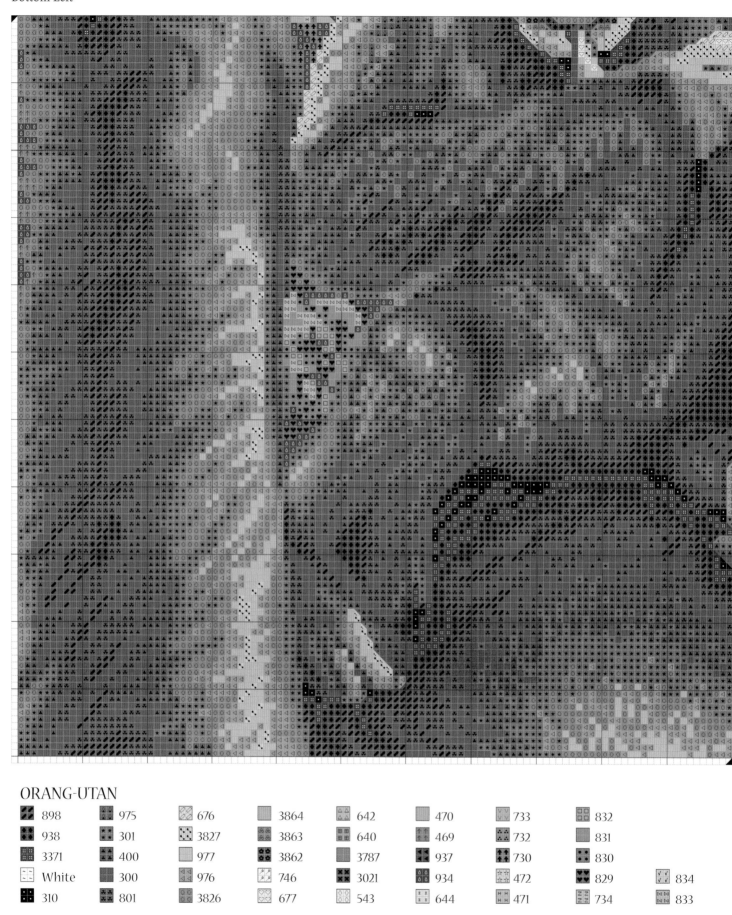

ORANG-UTAN

898	975	676	3864	642	470	733	832	
938	301	3827	3863	640	469	732	831	
3371	400	977	3862	3787	937	730	830	
White	300	976	746	934	472	829	834
310	801	3826	677	543	644	471	734	833

RHINOCEROS

There are five species of rhinoceros, two native to Africa and three to southern Asia – four of the five species are endangered, some critically so. This Indian rhinoceros, with its armour-plated appearance, looks like a relic from prehistoric times. It has deeply folded skin, with rivet-like lumps that give it a very distinctive form. It has only one horn and feeds mainly on grass. It is one of the most aquatic of the rhinos, wading and swimming with ease.

Rhinos are generally solitary, although females and young males will share territory and bathing pools without aggression. The males develop large, sharp, tusk-like incisors. When two strong males meet they use these to devastate their opponent when fighting over territory or a female. Sadly, these bouts often end in the death of one of them.

Armour-plated Survivor

Stitch count 108h x 140w
Design size 19.5 x 25.5cm (7¾ x 10in)

YOU WILL NEED

❋ 35.5 x 40.5cm (14 x 16in) light green 28-count linen
  (DMC code 772)
❋ DMC stranded cotton (floss) as listed in the chart key
  (1 skein of each colour)
❋ Tapestry needle size 24–26
❋ Suitable picture frame

1 Prepare your fabric and mark the centre point (see page 99). Work outwards from the centre of the fabric and the centre of the chart overleaf.

2 Work over two threads of linen, using two strands of stranded cotton (floss) for all cross stitches. Only whole cross stitches are used in the design.

3 Once all the stitching is complete, check for missed stitches, remove any guidelines and then mount and frame the picture (see page 102 for advice).

The armoured bulk of this magnificent creature is portrayed in this embroidery. The use of a light green fabric creates a balanced tone with the greys and browns of his hide, and also conveys the rhino's forest environment.

Rhinos have long been killed just for their horn, which is shaped into ornaments such as cups and daggers and also used in traditional Chinese medicine. The horn isn't made of hair, as was previously thought, but of keratin, the same protein that makes hair.

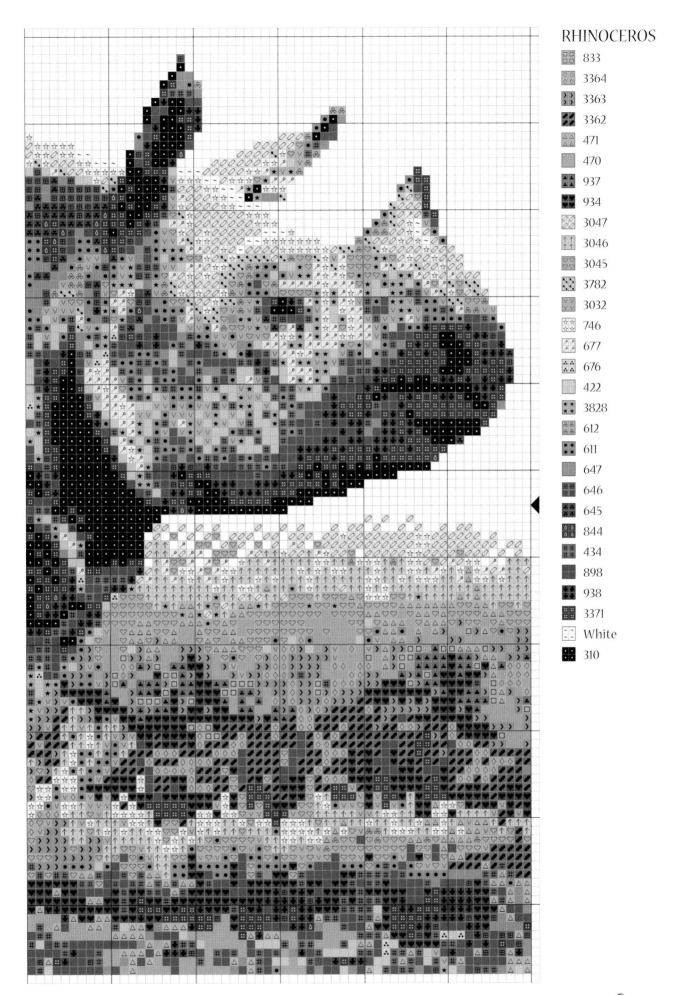

RHINOCEROS

833	
3364	
3363	
3362	
471	
470	
937	
934	
3047	
3046	
3045	
3782	
3032	
746	
677	
676	
422	
3828	
612	
611	
647	
646	
645	
844	
434	
898	
938	
3371	
White	
310	

BIRD OF PARADISE

At present there are 42 birds of paradise species – that we know of – and they can be found in eastern Indonesia, Papua New Guinea and eastern Australia. My design features the Lesser Bird of Paradise, totally absorbed in his elaborate mating display.

While nearly all of the female birds of paradise are brown and nondescript, the males have evolved the greatest variation of feather colour and form in the bird kingdom. The courtship displays of the males are truly extraordinary and everywhere seems to be a stage for them. They perform on the ground, with a plume of feathers draped over them like a cape or even hanging upside down from branches, with tails splayed like dishes or cascading in a fabulous waterfall of plumage.

Winged Angels

Stitch count 110h x 150w
Design size 20 x 27.3cm (7¾ x 10¾in)

YOU WILL NEED

※ 35.5 x 43.2cm (14 x 17in) white 14-count Aida
※ DMC stranded cotton (floss) as listed in the chart key
   (1 skein of each colour but 2 skeins of 3053)
※ Tapestry needle size 24–26
※ Suitable picture frame

1 Prepare your fabric and mark the centre point (see page 99). Work outwards from the centre of the fabric and the centre of the chart overleaf.

2 Work over one block of Aida, using two strands of stranded cotton (floss) for the whole cross stitches. For the eye work a French knot with two strands of black wound once around the needle.

3 Once all the stitching is complete, check for missed stitches, remove any guidelines and then mount and frame the picture (see page 102 for advice).

The arcing white and pale yellow cross stitches in this design create a sense of movement, where you can almost see the spectacular tail feathers shimmering and shining as the bird performs his mating dance.

In the 16th century there was a myth that these birds spent their entire life on the wing, like angels, falling to earth only when they died. The reason for this was the fact that the feet had been removed from all the specimens brought back to Europe.

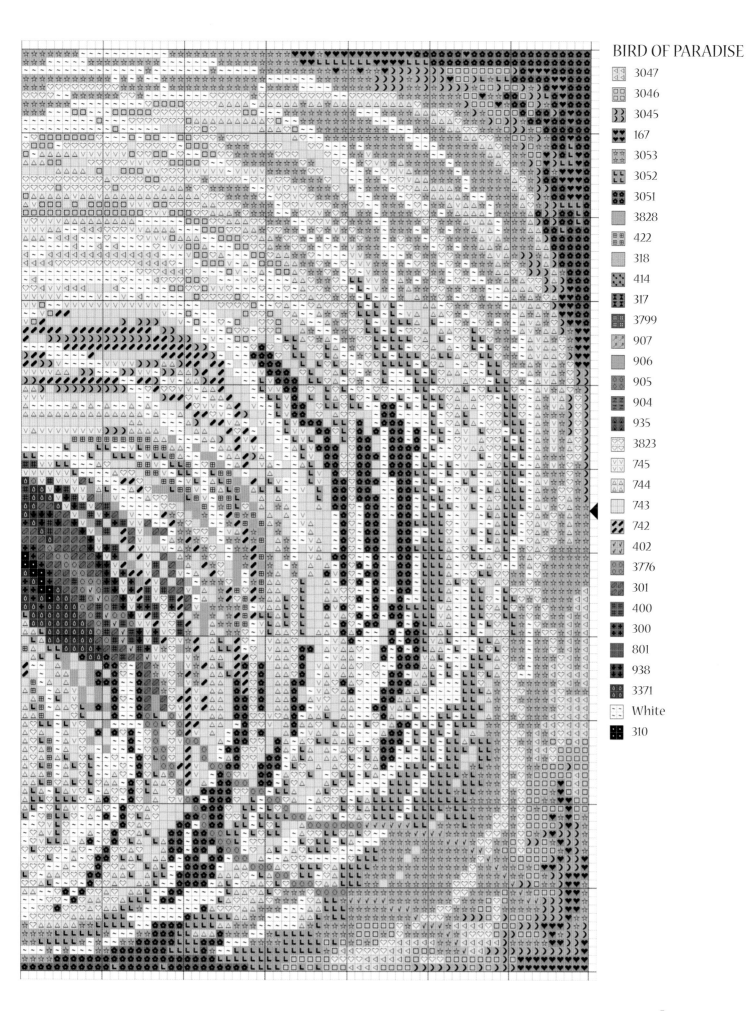

BIRD OF PARADISE

3047
3046
3045
167
3053
3052
3051
3828
422
318
414
317
3799
907
906
905
904
935
3823
745
744
743
742
402
3776
301
400
300
801
938
3371
White
310

BOA

Boas are snakes that can be found from Mexico to Argentina and on some of the Caribbean islands. The greatest variety live in tropical rainforests, where there is plenty of food. Many boas are nocturnal feeders and their diet includes lizards, birds, rats, squirrels, opossums and mongooses, which they kill by constriction.

Boas come in many forms, patterns and colours – from the black, tan and white Boa constrictor in my design, to bright emerald green. Many tree snakes are green or with brown patterns to break up and disguise their outlines. Some of their skin patterns even look like moss or lichens. Tree boas tend to be longer and slimmer than boas that live on the ground as this helps them slide through the branches.

Lithe Beauty

Stitch count 125h x 110w
Design size 22.7 x 20cm (9 x 7¾in)

YOU WILL NEED

※ 38 x 35.5cm (15 x 14in) cream 14-count Aida
※ DMC stranded cotton (floss) as listed in the chart key (1 skein of each colour)
※ Tapestry needle size 24–26
※ Suitable picture frame

1 Prepare your fabric and mark the centre point (see page 99). Work outwards from the centre of the fabric and the centre of the chart overleaf.

2 Work over one block of Aida, using two strands of stranded cotton (floss) for full and three-quarter cross stitches. For the eye highlight work a French knot with one strand of white.

3 Once all the stitching is complete, check for missed stitches, remove any guidelines and then mount and frame the picture (see page 102 for advice).

Boas vary in size but usually grow to 1.3–3.7m (4–12ft) long. The longest snake in the world is the reticulated python, which can grow up to 10m (32ft) long; the smallest is the tiny thread snake at only 10.2cm (4in).

Boas make great use of trees to move around in search of prey and as perches. This design shows the snake in a characteristic coiled pose, with markings clearly shown.

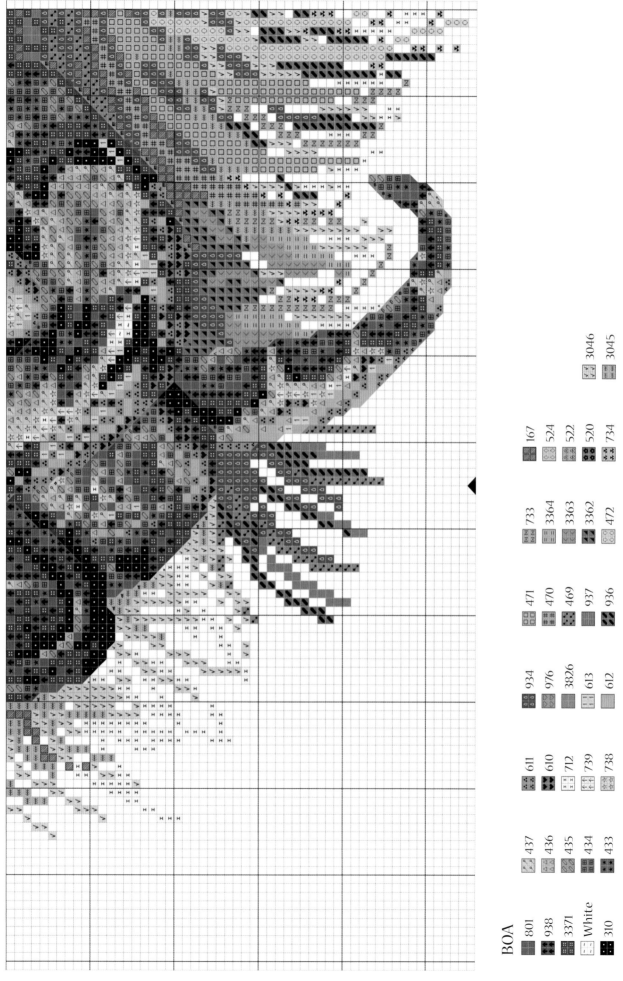

BOA

	801		437		611		934		471		733		167
	938		436		610		976		470		3364		524
	3371		435		712		3826		469		3363		522
	White		434		739		613		937		3362		520
	310		433		738		612		936		472		734

| | 3046 |
| | 3045 |

Boa 65

JAGUAR

The jaguar is the top predator of all the rainforest cats and can be found in rainforests, swamps and savannas of central South America and Mexico. A solitary cat, it was once found in North America but was driven out by persecution and loss of habitat.

An expert climber and swimmer, and with the most powerful jaws and teeth of all cats, the jaguar uses stealth, strength and cunning to catch its prey. Jaguars are also water lovers and their diet includes fish and small alligators, as well as land-based peccary (a wild pig) and capybara (a large rodent). Its dappled coat provides the perfect camouflage, allowing it to blend away in the mottled light of the forest floor.

Dappled Beauty

Stitch count 150h x 200w
Design size 27.3 x 36.3cm (10¾ x 14¼in)

YOU WILL NEED

※ 43.2 x 53.5cm (17 x 21in) white 14-count Aida
※ DMC stranded cotton (floss) as listed in the chart key (1 skein of each colour but 2 skeins of white and 924 and 3 skeins of 310)
※ Tapestry needle size 24–26
※ Suitable picture frame

1 Prepare your fabric and mark the centre point (see page 99). Work outwards from the centre of the fabric and the chart on pages 68–71.

2 Work over one block of Aida, using two strands of stranded cotton (floss) for cross stitch.

3 Once all the stitching is complete, check for missed stitches, remove any guidelines and then mount and frame the picture (see page 102 for advice).

At home in water as much as on dry land this stunning cat melts away in the ripples of water, his dappled spots resembling the pebbles on the riverbed

Some Amazonian tribes claim to have jaguar ancestry and mimic the cat's camouflage with face paint. These 'cat-people' tattoo their faces and pierce their lips and noses with spines to represent whiskers and file their teeth to present a more feline appearance.

JAGUAR

3787	822	801	3768	370	422	500	3813	647	3072
3021	644	938	924	830	3828	928	503	646	648
White	642	3371	934	677	420	927	502	645	
310	640	3866	372	676	869	926	501	844	

Top Left

3787	822		
3021	644		
White	642		
310	640		

801	422	370	3768
938	3828	830	924
3371	420	677	934
3866	869	676	372

500	3813	647	3072
928	503	646	648
927	502	645	
926	501	844	

Top Right

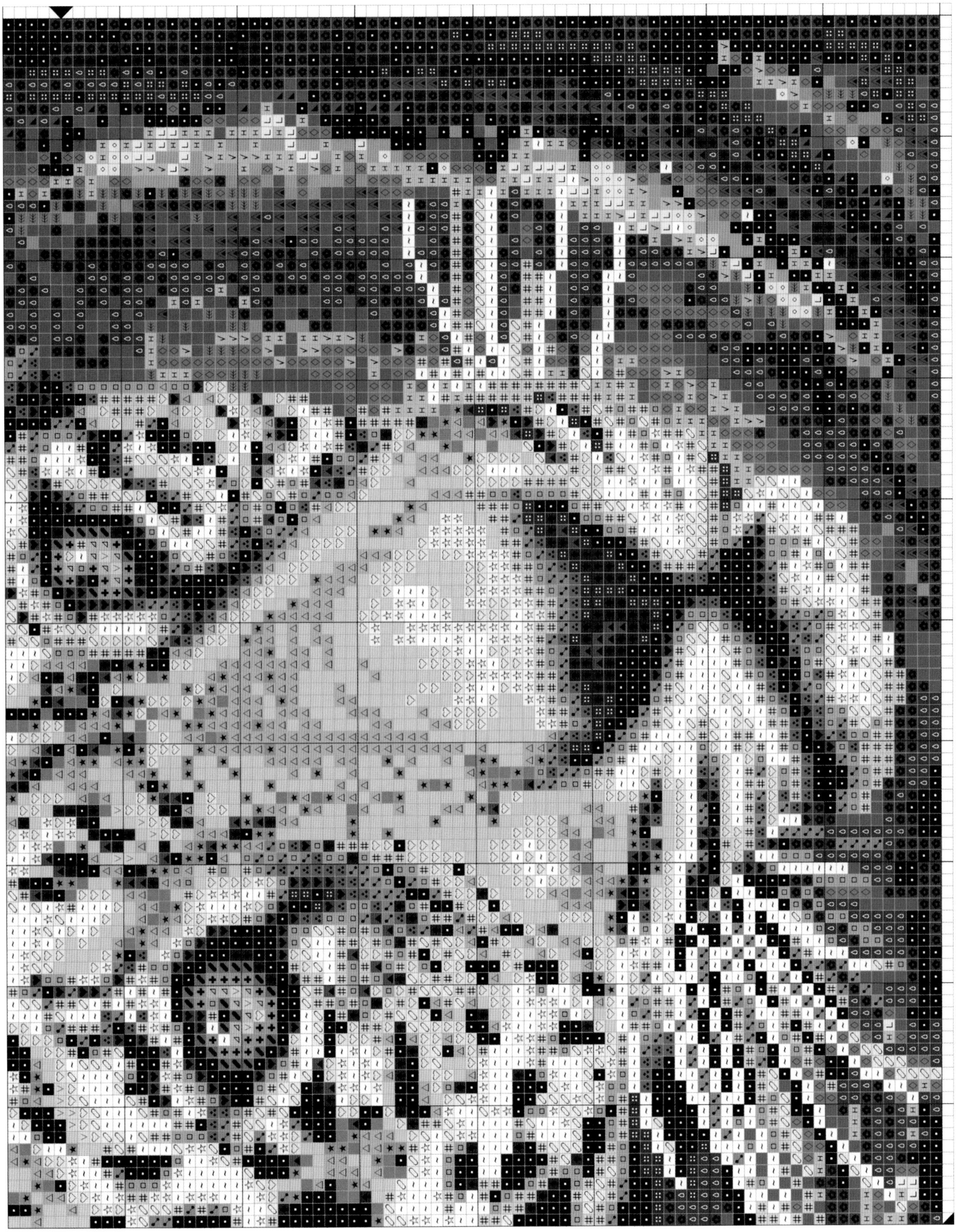

Bottom Right

BUTTERFLIES

Butterflies can be found all over the world except in very cold or very arid areas and there are an estimated 17,500 species. This stunning embroidery shows a mass of beautifully coloured butterflies from various jungle regions – 23 in total.

Butterflies spend much time feeding, mostly on flower nectar, and worldwide play an important role as pollinators. They also take nourishment from pollen, tree sap, rotting fruit and dung. Time is also spent basking, where the wings are oriented to gather heat from the sun. Many tropical butterflies darken in colour during the wet season, possibly to help protect them from predators. Delicate in form, jewel-coloured and with a fascinating life cycle, butterflies are nature at its best.

Jewels of the Air

Stitch count 110h x 150w
Design size 20 x 27.3cm (7¾ x 10¾in)

YOU WILL NEED

※ 35.5 x 43cm (14 x 17in) black 14-count Aida
※ DMC stranded cotton (floss) as listed in the chart key (1 skein of each colour but 2 skeins of 310)
※ Tapestry needle size 24–26
※ Suitable picture frame

1 Prepare your fabric and mark the centre point (see page 99). Work outwards from the centre of the fabric and chart.

2 Work over one Aida block, using two strands of stranded cotton (floss) for full and three-quarter cross stitches. Work the backstitch with one strand of black (shown in grey on the chart) for the eye detail and 905, 906 and 3823 for the butterfly details. For antennae details work French knots with one strand of 3823 would once around the needle.

3 Once stitching is complete, check for missed stitches, remove guidelines and mount and frame (see page 102).

Within this design there are 23 individual butterflies. You can stitch the whole design or just one butterfly. For butterflies with only one wing showing, you can stitch the whole butterfly by reversing the wing shown (use a photocopier to reverse the design).

Butterflies' wings are covered with tiny scales. Wings that show black and brown colours have scales pigmented with melanin, but wings that are blue, green, red and iridescent are the result of light being scattered by the crystal structure of the scales.

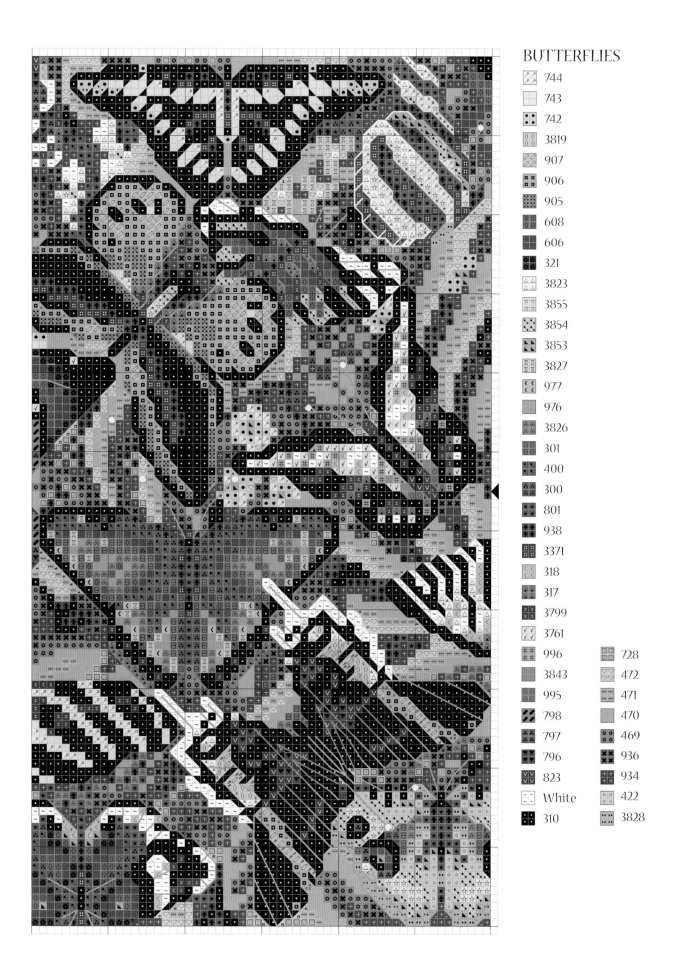

BUTTERFLIES

Symbol	Color	Symbol	Color
	744		
	743		
	742		
	3819		
	907		
	906		
	905		
	608		
	606		
	321		
	3823		
	3855		
	3854		
	3853		
	3827		
	977		
	976		
	3826		
	301		
	400		
	300		
	801		
	938		
	3371		
	318		
	317		
	3799		
	3761		
	996		728
	3843		472
	995		471
	798		470
	797		469
	796		936
	823		934
	White		422
	310		3828

SCARLET MACAW

Macaws are perhaps the most well known of all the birds in a tropical forest. They are the largest birds in the parrot family and are native to central and tropical South America and Mexico. Most prefer rainforest for their habitat, although some favour woodland or savanna-type habitats. There are now 23 species of macaw, classified into six genera.

Highly sociable in the wild and stunning in their variety of colours, macaws flock in large noisy groups to gather clay from river banks for the minerals they need. They eat fruit and nuts and gnaw on various objects. In the wild, their average life span is around 50 years. Scarlet macaws in particular are sought as pets, due to their striking colouring, intelligence and mimicry skills.

Master of Mimicry

Stitch count 120h x 160w
Design size 22 x 29cm (8¾ x 11½in)

YOU WILL NEED

※ 46 x 38cm (15 x 18in) sky blue 14-count Aida
※ DMC stranded cotton (floss) as listed in the chart key (1 skein of each colour)
※ Tapestry needle size 24–26
※ Suitable picture frame

1 Prepare your fabric and mark the centre point (see page 99). Work outwards from the centre of the fabric and the centre of the chart overleaf.

2 Work over one block of Aida, using two strands of stranded cotton (floss) for full and three-quarter cross stitches. Work the backstitch with one strand of black for the eye detail.

3 Once all the stitching is complete, check for missed stitches, remove any guidelines and then mount and frame the picture (see page 102 for advice).

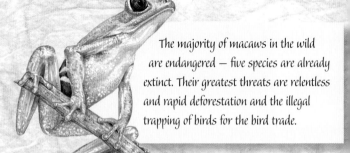

The majority of macaws in the wild are endangered – five species are already extinct. Their greatest threats are relentless and rapid deforestation and the illegal trapping of birds for the bird trade.

This head study shows the true beauty of a stunning scarlet macaw, with his strong seed-crushing beak, bright intelligent eye and fiery red neck feathers. This is truly one of the most magnificent of all the tropical birds.

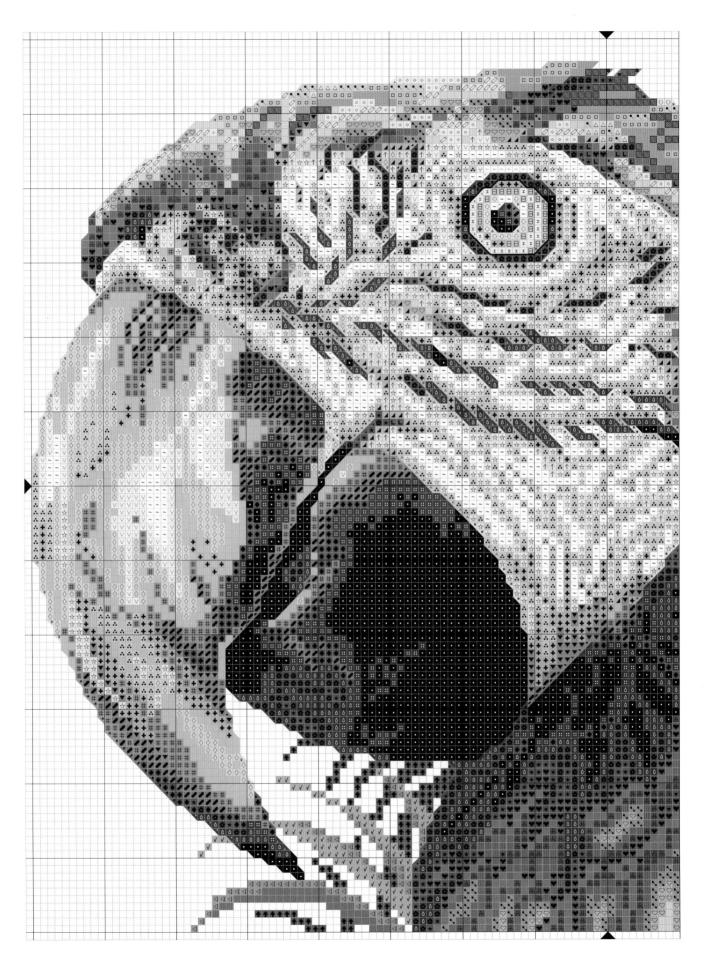

SCARLET MACAW

Symbol	Color
✖✖	935
■	3345
◁◁	3346
✓✓	3347
◣◣	3064
↑↑	950
✦✦	3033
⬡⬡	3782
✚✚	3032
▼▼	3790
▦▦	3348
◌◌	772
I I	3078
L L	433
★★	801
▦▦	938
◢◢	3371
△△	165
⦂⦂	3819
□□	166
▨	581
▦▦	580
◇◇	744
▨▨	743
▨	742
⬚⬚	741
⦂⦂	970
▦	947
▨	900
▨	301
▼▼	400
∨∨	762
◇◇	415
▨	318
✚✚	414
◢◢	317
✦✦	413
▦▦	3799
⌐⌐	White
✦✦	310

CHAMELEON

Most of the 160 or so species of chameleon live in Africa and Madagascar. They have an amazing ability to change their colour and blend in with their surroundings. This helps them to capture prey and communicate with other chameleons for mating and territorial displays. They have extremely long tongues, about 50cm (20in), and use these to trap insects and small birds. They are also able to rotate their eyes independently, to keep watch on two different directions.

My embroidery features Oustalet's chameleon, which is a large creature with a stout body. Its normal colour is green with yellow stripes and random darker spots. The males of many chameleon species have different head sizes and ornamentations, including horns.

Champion of Camouflage

Stitch count 145h x 110w
Design size 26.5 x 20cm (10½ x 7¾in)

YOU WILL NEED

* 43.2 x 35.5cm (17 x 14in) yellow green 28-count linen (DMC code 772)
* DMC stranded cotton (floss) as listed in the chart key (1 skein of each colour)
* Tapestry needle size 24–26
* Suitable picture frame

1 Prepare your fabric and mark the centre point (see page 99). Work outwards from the centre of the fabric and the centre of the chart overleaf.

2 Work over two threads of linen, using two strands of stranded cotton (floss) for full and three-quarter cross stitches. Work the backstitch with one strand of white around the eye, black for the eye detail and grey 646 for the mouth line.

3 Once all the stitching is complete, check for missed stitches, remove any guidelines and then mount and frame the picture (see page 102 for advice).

In Madagascar, the chameleon is regarded with great suspicion because of the fact that its eyes can look in different directions at the same time. People believe that the creature can see into the past and the future and so it is considered an evil omen.

With the curl of the tail and subtle shading this chameleon blends away into the foliage. You can almost feel him waiting for an insect to pass his way so he can flip out his tongue at lightning speed and bring his prey to a sticky end.

CHAMELEON

165	580	829
772	581	3051
White	166	906
310	3819	907

3825	3022	3348
833	3023	677
831	3024	436
830	922	646

676	680
3345	729
3346	
3347	

SLOTH

The sloth must be one of the most unusual creatures on the planet. They spend much of their time in trees, usually hanging upside down, using their long limbs to move around – *very* slowly. They can be found in Central and South America and their diet consists of buds, tender shoots and leaves, although they will also eat insects, small lizards and carrion.

Each day the sloth makes its way down to the jungle floor from high in the trees to defecate on the ground. The energy required for this daily excursion, must make the sloth one of the most considerate animals in the jungle. The ultra-slow movements of the sloth conserves energy, as does sleeping, in which state they spend 15–18 hours every day.

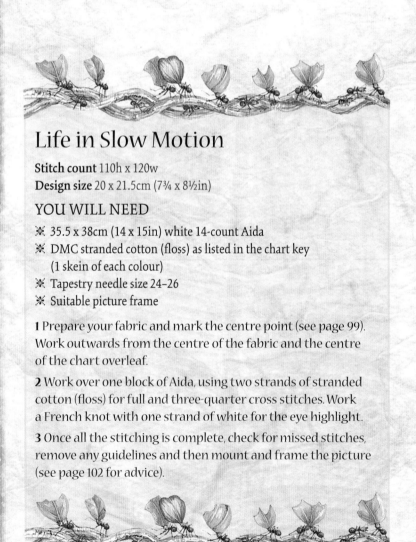

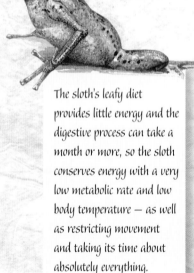

Life in Slow Motion

Stitch count 110h x 120w
Design size 20 x 21.5cm (7¾ x 8½in)

YOU WILL NEED

✳ 35.5 x 38cm (14 x 15in) white 14-count Aida
✳ DMC stranded cotton (floss) as listed in the chart key
   (1 skein of each colour)
✳ Tapestry needle size 24–26
✳ Suitable picture frame

1 Prepare your fabric and mark the centre point (see page 99). Work outwards from the centre of the fabric and the centre of the chart overleaf.

2 Work over one block of Aida, using two strands of stranded cotton (floss) for full and three-quarter cross stitches. Work a French knot with one strand of white for the eye highlight.

3 Once all the stitching is complete, check for missed stitches, remove any guidelines and then mount and frame the picture (see page 102 for advice).

The sloth's leafy diet provides little energy and the digestive process can take a month or more, so the sloth conserves energy with a very low metabolic rate and low body temperature — as well as restricting movement and taking its time about absolutely everything.

My design
shows the sloth in a
characteristic upside down
position. Most mammals' hair
grows towards the extremities
but because a sloth spends so
much time with their legs above
their body this hair direction is
reversed, to protect them
from the elements.

SLOTH

738		3047	
739		3046	
712		3045	
453		780	
452		783	
451		677	
433		3348	
801		3347	
898		3346	
938		3345	
3371		3013	
3866		3012	
3033		3011	
3782		936	
3032		934	
3790		414	
3781		413	
3021		3799	
White		3828	
310		422	

PEACOCK

The fabulous bird in this design is an Indian peafowl, though the male is so spectacular and memorable that we usually use the word peacock to describe males and females. It can be found all over the Indian subcontinent and is the national bird of India.

From the tip of its beak to the end of its gorgeous tail, the peacock is an exotic beauty. The iridescent colouring and the well-known eye spot on the tail feathers makes this one of the best known jungle birds. Some people consider the eye-marked feathers unlucky and will not bring them into the house, but for artists and designers they are an inspiration.

Proud and Perfect

Stitch count 220h x 150w
Design size 40 x 27.3cm (15¾ x 10¾in)

YOU WILL NEED

❋ 56 x 43.2cm (22 x 17in) sky blue 28-count linen (DMC code 762)
❋ DMC stranded cotton (floss) as listed in the chart key
   (1 skein of each colour)
❋ DMC Light Effects threads as listed in chart key
   (1 skein of each colour)
❋ Tapestry needle size 24–26
❋ Suitable picture frame

1 Prepare your fabric and mark the centre point (see page 99). Work outwards from the centre of the fabric and chart on pages 90–93.

2 Work over two threads of linen, using two strands of stranded cotton (floss) for full and three-quarter cross stitches. Work the backstitch with one strand of 890 for the tail feather detail and 939 (shown in black on the chart) for the head feather detail (and in parts of the tail). Use one strand doubled in the needle when working with the metallic threads – see page 99 for advice. For the eye highlight work a French knot with two strands of white wound once around the needle.

3 Once all the stitching is complete, check for missed stitches, remove any guidelines and then mount and frame the picture (see page 102 for advice).

The so-called 'tail' or 'train' of an adult peacock has an average of 200 tail feathers, which are shed and re-grown annually. Of these 200, 170 are 'eye' feathers (also called ocellations) and 30 are 'T' feathers, which border the end of the train.

The iridescent colouring of the peacock's feathers is achieved by using metallic thread. Further realism is brought to the scene by draping the tail feathers over the edge of the frame, as if the bird were in a window open to a sunlit glade.

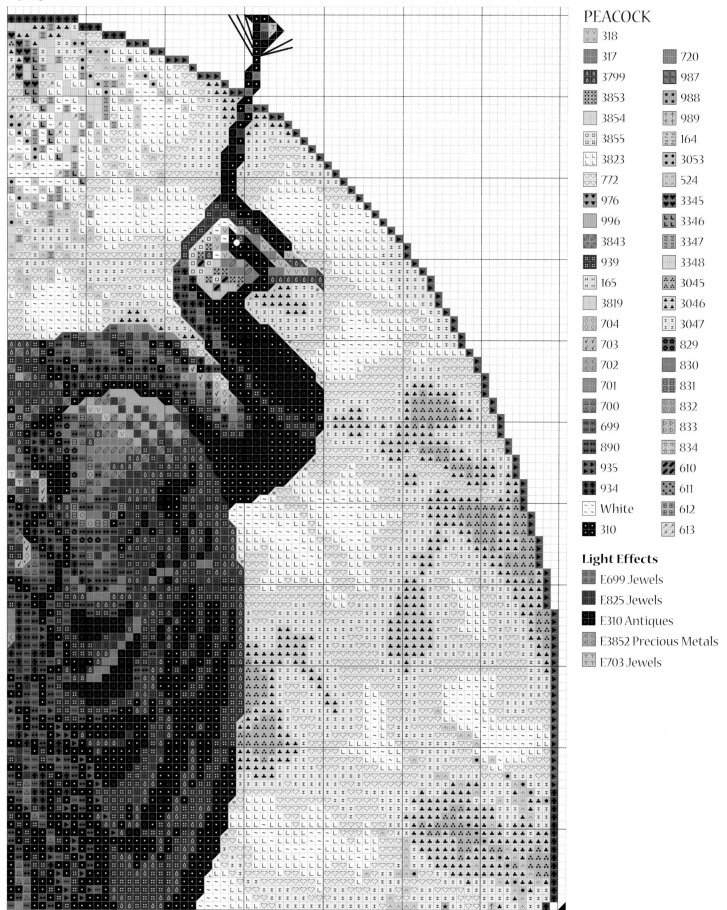

PEACOCK

318			
317		720	
3799		987	
3853		988	
3854		989	
3855		164	
3823		3053	
772		524	
976		3345	
996		3346	
3843		3347	
939		3348	
165		3045	
3819		3046	
704		3047	
703		829	
702		830	
701		831	
700		832	
699		833	
890		834	
935		610	
934		611	
White		612	
310		613	

Light Effects

E699 Jewels

E825 Jewels

E310 Antiques

E3852 Precious Metals

E703 Jewels

Bottom Right

PEACOCK

318			
317		720	
3799		987	
3853		988	
3854		989	
3855		164	
3823		3053	
772		524	
976		3345	
996		3346	
3843		3347	
939		3348	
165		3045	
3819		3046	
704		3047	
703		829	
702		830	
701		831	
700		832	
699		833	
890		834	
935		610	
934		611	
White		612	
310		613	

Light Effects

E699 Jewels

E825 Jewels

E310 Antiques

E3852 Precious Metals

E703 Jewels

AMAZONIAN TRIBESMAN

This design features Kayapo Indians from the Amazonian lowlands, performing a traditional war dance to enlist the protection of the forest spirits. Many tribes have claimed jaguar ancestry and some hunters mimic the jaguar's camouflage with blotched face paint or tattoos, piercing their lips and nostrils with spines to represent whiskers. These remarkable cat-people hunt with cudgels studded with jaguar teeth and file their own teeth to accentuate their feline appearance.

The tribes of the Amazon have survived by blending into and becoming part of the jungle as much as the plants and animals. However, almost 100 Amazonian Indian tribes have disappeared since the early 1900s, and with them has vanished their folklore and medicinal knowledge of the plants that surrounded them.

Dancing Forest Spirit

Stitch count 150h x 110w
Design size 27.3 x 20cm (10¾ x 7¾in)

YOU WILL NEED

※ 43.2 x 35.5cm (17 x 14in) blue 28-count linen (DMC code 3840)
※ DMC stranded cotton (floss) as listed in the chart key (1 skein of each colour)
※ Glass seed beads, one pack each of the following colours – white, red, medium gold, light gold, dark blue, medium blue and light blue
※ Tapestry needle size 24–26
※ Suitable picture frame

1 Prepare your fabric and mark the centre point (see page 99). Work outwards from the centre of the fabric and the chart overleaf.

2 Work over two threads of linen, using two strands of stranded cotton (floss) for full and three-quarter cross stitches. Work the backstitch with one strand of black for the face detail. Add beads in place of the cross stitch as follows. Use white beads on armbands and eardrops. Use red beads on the pendant. Use gold beads on the pendant and necklace. Use blue beads on the armbands and necklace. (See page 101 for a close-up photo of these bead colours.)

3 Once all stitching is complete, check for missed stitches, remove any guidelines and then mount and frame the picture (see page 102).

The Kayapo Indians live in balance with their environment and are highly evolved ecologically. The jungle surrounding them is used for practical and medicinal purposes and they cultivate many plants using biological pest controls.

The Kayapo Indians adorn their arms and legs and wear a head-dress of parrot feathers for their dance for the forest spirits. The use of brightly coloured seed beads in the design highlights these decorations and creates texture.

AMAZONIAN TRIBESMAN

801	950	414
938	3064	317
3371	3772	413
White	632	3799
310	300	3774

972	900	825
907	3078	606
906	727	970
905	726	947
904	725	946

3033	422	869
3821	985	420
3852	934	3828
813	3032	
826	3782	

WORKBOX

This section gives you all the information you will need to produce perfect cross stitch embroidery and successfully recreate the projects in this book. There is advice on materials and equipment, embroidery techniques, stitches and making up methods.

MATERIALS AND EQUIPMENT

This short section describes the basic materials and equipment you will need to stitch the cross stitch designs in this book.

Fabrics

Most of the designs in this book have been worked on Aida fabric, which is stitched over one block. Where a specific colour of DMC fabric has been used the code number is given. The main size used is 14 blocks or threads to 1in (2.5cm), often called 14-count. Some designs use an evenweave fabric such as linen, which should be worked over two threads. The same design stitched on fabrics of different counts will work up as different sizes. The larger the count, the more threads per 1in (2.5cm), therefore the smaller the finished design, and vice versa. Each project lists the type of fabric used, giving the thread count and fabric name. All DMC threads and fabrics are available from good needlework shops (see Suppliers for details).

Threads

If you want your designs to look the same as those shown in the photographs, you need to use the colours and threads listed for each project. I've used DMC stranded cotton (floss) but you could use other threads ranges – ask for conversion tables at your local needlecraft store. Some projects could be stitched with tapestry wool (yarn) instead, especially those worked in full cross stitch.

It is best to keep threads tidy and manageable with thread organizers and project cards. Cut the threads to equal lengths and loop them into project cards with the thread shade code and colour key symbol noted at the side. This will prevent threads becoming tangled and codes being lost.

Stranded cotton (floss) This is the most widely used embroidery thread and is available in hundreds of colours, including silver and gold metallic. It is made from six strands twisted together to form a thick thread, which can be used whole or split into its thinner strands. The type of fabric used will determine how many strands of thread you use: most of the designs in this book use two strands for cross stitch and one for backstitch.

Metallic threads Some DMC Light Effects threads have been used in the peacock design to bring a sparkle to the bird's plumage. These threads are six-stranded and are used in the same way as stranded cotton, usually two strands for cross stitch and one for backstitch. See opposite for advice on using metallic threads.

Needles

Stitch your designs using a tapestry needle, which has a large eye and a blunt end to prevent damage to the fabric. Choose a size of needle that will slide easily through the fabric holes without distorting or enlarging them. When sewing on seed beads use a beading needle, as this is thin enough to thread through the hole in the bead.

Scissors

You will need sharp embroidery scissors for cutting threads and good dressmaking shears for cutting fabric.

Embroidery Frames

Your work will be easier to handle and stitches will be kept flat and smooth if you mount your fabric on an embroidery hoop or frame, which will accommodate the whole design. Bind the outer ring of a hoop with a white bias tape to prevent it from marking the fabric. This will also keep the fabric taut and prevent it from slipping whilst you are working. Avoid placing a hoop over worked cross stitches as it will distort and flatten them.

BASIC TECHNIQUES

The following techniques and tips will help you attain a professional finish by showing you how to prepare for work, work the stitches and care for your embroidery.

Preparing Fabric

Spending a little time preparing your embroidery fabric for work is a good idea, helping to avoid mistakes and produce superior finished results.

Fabric sizes Make sure you are using the correct size of fabric by checking the stitch count (the number of stitches across the height and width of the design) and design size given with each project. Each project gives the finished size of a design when worked on the recommended fabric, together with the amount of fabric needed. The overall fabric size should be at least 8–12.5cm (3–5in) larger than the finished size of the design to allow for turnings or seam allowances when mounting the work or making it up. To prevent fabric from fraying, machine stitch around the edges or bind with tape. Measurements are given in metric with imperial equivalent in brackets. Always use either metric or imperial – do not mix the two.

Centre point Starting your stitching from the centre point of the fabric ensures you will have enough fabric all round the design. To find the centre point, tack (baste) a row of stitches horizontally and vertically from the centre of each side of the fabric. These lines correspond to the arrows at the side of each chart and will cross at the centre point. Remove any tacking once the embroidery is complete.

Using Charts

All the designs in this book use DMC embroidery fabrics and stranded cotton (floss). The colours and symbols shown on the chart keys correspond to DMC shade codes. Each coloured square on the chart represents one complete cross stitch and some squares also have a symbol. The colours and symbols correspond to those in the key beside each chart. A small triangle in a corner of a grid square represents a three-quarter cross stitch. French knots are shown by a coloured dot – the project instructions specify what thread shade to use. Solid coloured lines indicate backstitch or long stitch – refer to the project instructions for details. The optional use of beads on a design will be in the instructions and will also specify which colours they replace.

Small black arrows at the side of a chart indicate the centre, and by lining these up you can find the centre point. Some of the charts are spread over four pages with the key repeated on each double page. Work systematically so you read the chart accurately and

avoid mistakes. Constantly check your progress against the chart and count the stitches as you go. If your sight is poor you may find it helpful to enlarge a chart on a colour photocopier.

Changing Design Sizes

The main projects have been worked on 14-count Aida or 28-count evenweave and the finished design sizes and stitch counts are given in the project instructions. You can change the finished size of a design by working it on fabric with a higher or lower stitch count. To find the finished size divide the stitch count by the 'count' of the fabric you wish to use. Always be generous with fabric allowances, as you can trim the excess off. For larger designs, such as pictures, add at least 12.5cm (5in) more than the finished design size all round.

Using Metallic Threads

When working with metallic threads, stitch with shorter lengths to avoid excessive wear on the thread –– about 30.5cm (12in). As these threads are springier than stranded cotton, it is helpful to thread the needle as shown in the diagram below, which will keep the thread secure as you stitch.

Fig 1 *To thread metallic threads, form a loop of thread and thread the needle with the loop. Pass the loop over the point of the needle and pull back so the loop tightens*

Washing and Pressing Embroidery

If your work has become grubby during stitching, gently hand wash it in warm water using a mild liquid detergent. Do not rub or wring. If necessary, use a soft nail brush on stubborn marks. Rinse in clean water, place the damp fabric on a clean white towel and leave to dry on a flat surface.

When ironing cross stitch embroidery, do not iron directly on your embroidery as this will flatten the stitches and remove the sheen from the threads. Lay the work face down on a thick, clean white towel, cover with a fine cloth and press carefully with a medium iron, taking extra care with beads or metallic threads.

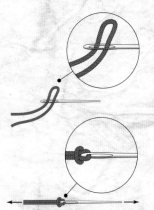

STITCHES

This section shows how to work the stitches used in the book. When following these instructions, note that stitching is over one block of Aida fabric or two threads of evenweave/linen.

Starting and Finishing Thread

To start off your first length of thread, make a knot at one end and push the needle through to the back of the fabric, about 2.5cm (1in) from your starting point, leaving the knot on the right side. Stitch towards the knot, securing the thread at the back of the fabric as you go (see diagram below). When the thread is secure, cut off the knot.

To finish off a thread or start new threads, simply weave the thread into the back of several stitches and then trim the end.

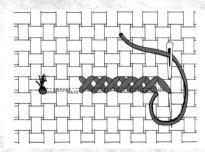

Fig 2 *Starting to stitch*

Backstitch

Backstitch is indicated on the charts by a solid coloured line. It is worked around areas of completed cross stitches to add definition, or on top of stitches to add detail.

To work backstitch (see Fig 3), put the needle through the hole in the fabric at 1 and back through at 2. For the next stitch, put the needle through at 3, then push to the back at 1, and repeat the process to make the next stitch. If working backstitch on an evenweave fabric, work each backstitch over two threads.

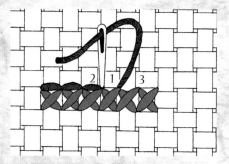

Fig 3 *Working backstitch*

Cross Stitch

Each coloured square on a chart represents one complete cross stitch. Cross stitch is worked in two easy stages. Start by working one diagonal stitch over one block of Aida (Fig 4) or two threads of evenweave (Fig 5), and then work a second diagonal stitch over the first stitch, but in the opposite direction to form a cross.

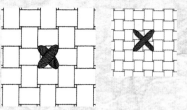

Fig 4 *A single cross stitch on Aida fabric*   **Fig 5** *A single cross stitch on evenweave fabric*

Cross stitches can be worked in rows if you have a large area to cover. Work a row of half cross stitches in one direction and then back in the opposite direction with the diagonal stitches to complete each cross. The upper stitches of all the crosses should lie in the same direction to produce a neat effect (Fig 6).

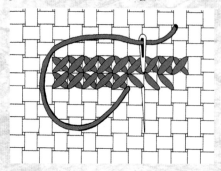

Fig 6 *Working cross stitch in rows, in two journeys*

Half Cross Stitch

This stitch may be used if you work a design on canvas in tapestry wool (yarn), replacing whole cross stitches with half stitches. A half cross stitch is simply one half of a cross stitch, with the diagonal facing the same way as the upper stitches of each complete cross stitch (Fig 7).

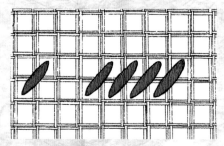

Fig 7 *Working half cross stitch*

Three-Quarter Cross Stitch

A small coloured triangle taking up half a chart square represents a three-quarter cross stitch. Forming this stitch is less accurate on Aida than on evenweave because the centre of the Aida block has to be pierced.

Work the first half of a cross stitch in the normal way, then work the second diagonal stitch in the opposite corner but insert the needle at the centre of the cross, forming three-quarters of the complete stitch (Fig 8). A square showing two smaller coloured triangles in opposite corners indicates that two three-quarter cross stitches will have to be worked back to back, sharing holes.

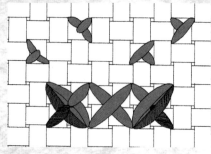

Fig 8 *Working three-quarter cross stitch*

French Knot

This is a small knot used for details, and eye highlights, and is indicated on charts by coloured dots.

To work a French knot, bring the needle through to the front of the fabric, just above the point you want the stitch placed. Wind the thread once around the needle and, holding the twisted thread firmly, insert the needle a little away from its starting position (Fig 9). Two tips for working French knots: never rush them and never go back into the same point where your thread came up or your knot will pull through to the back.

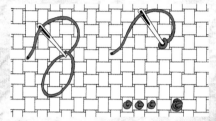

Fig 9 *Working French knots*

Long Stitch

These are used to work some animal whiskers and are indicated on charts by a straight coloured line – refer to the instructions for the colour. Work long stitches on top of cross stitches (see Fig 10).

To work long stitch, pull the needle through the fabric at the point indicated on the chart and push it through at the other end shown on the chart, to make a long, straight stitch on top of the fabric. Repeat for the next stitch, carrying the thread across the back of the fabric to the next starting point.

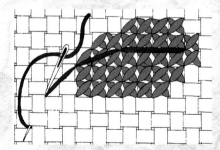

Fig 10 *Working long stitch*

Adding Beads

Seed beads can be added to cross stitch or sewn in place to replace cross stitches. The Amazonian Tribesman has areas of beads used instead of cross stitches to create texture in the design. I used DMC beads but if you cannot obtain these use beads from another manufacturer such as Mill Hill – the picture here shows the bead colours in detail so you can match them.

Use a beading needle to sew on seed beads and match the thread colour to the bead colour. Attach the bead using half cross stitch, with the stitches running in the same direction so the beads lie in neat rows on the fabric.

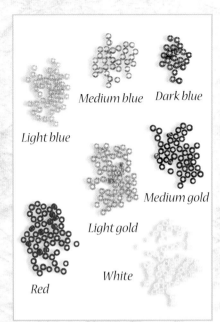

The bead colours used in the Amazonian Tribesman design (page 94)

MAKING UP

This section describes how to make up the embroideries as illustrated, although the designs are simple to adapt and use in many different ways – see Jungle Inspirations pages 6–9. When making up any item, a 1.3cm (½in) seam allowance has been used.

MOUNTING AND FRAMING

It really is best to take larger pictures to a professional framer, who will be able to stretch the fabric correctly and cut any surrounding mounts accurately. If, however, you prefer to mount and frame yourself you will need a mitre box for cutting mitred corners on frames, some panel pins, a suitable saw, some hardboard (or thick card) and mount board. When choosing mount board and a frame, it is best to take your finished work with you, to get an idea of what the end result will be.

1 Mount your embroidery on to thin hardboard or card and fasten by lacing it around the card or by stapling.

2 Decide on the frame size you require and carefully cut your frame pieces to the correct size. Use panel pins to fix them together.

3 Using a mount cutter or a craft or Stanley knife, cut your mount board to the required depth. Place the mount board into the frame, then the embroidery.

4 Finally, cut hardboard to size for the backing and wedge in with metal clips or tape in place.

USING READY-MADE ITEMS

Many of the projects in the book can be displayed in ready-made items such as firescreens and footstools, while the smaller designs in Jungle Inspirations (pages 6–9) can be used in cards, trinket boxes and other smaller items. There are various manufacturers supplying such items (see Suppliers).

Smaller pieces of embroidery can be backed with an iron-on interfacing (such as Vilene) to firm up the fabric and prevent wrinkling, and then be mounted in the item following the manufacturer's instructions.

MOUNTING WORK IN CARDS

Double-fold cards with an aperture are readily available for embroidery (see Suppliers). Trim the embroidery so it is slightly larger than the card aperture and use double-sided tape inside the card around the aperture, pressing the embroidery on to the tape, making sure it is central within the card aperture. The Framecraft cards I use already have this tape in place.

MAKING UP A CUSHION

These making up instructions are for the cushion shown on page 7, which has a finished size of 34.3 x 43.2cm (13½ x 17in), excluding frill. You could omit the frill if desired. You will need: your embroidered Aida band of 34.3cm (13½in); complementary fabric 1.5m (1½yd) for the cushion; fabric for the frill 12.7cm (5in) wide x 4m (4¼yd) long (approx); matching sewing thread and a cushion pad to fit.

1 From your complementary fabric cut one piece 36.8 x 45.7cm (14½ x 18in) and two pieces 29.2 x 36.8cm (11½ x 14½in). Seam allowances are 1.3cm (½in).

2 Pin the embroidered Aida band across the large rectangle of fabric about 9cm (3½in) from the right-hand edge. Tack (baste) and then machine stitch in place. Make sure the edge of the stitching matches up to the seam allowance. Turn a hem on one side of each of the two back pieces.

3 For the frill, stitch the strip together to form a circle, fold in half lengthways and press the entire length. Run two rows of tacking all the way around the circle (as drawstrings) on the unfolded edge. Lay the front of the cushion on a flat surface facing upwards, place the frill with the raw edges together and the frill pointing inwards. Gather the frill evenly, pinning as you go all the way around, and then tack into place.

4 Lay the back pieces over the front and frill, raw edges matching and the hemmed sides overlapping in the centre. Pin and then tack all the layers together. Machine stitch all three layers together. Turn the right side out and insert your cushion pad.

Stitching Tips

✳ Steam press your embroidery fabric before stitching to remove any stubborn creases.

✳ Mount fabric on to an embroidery frame or hoop to keep stitches smooth and flat.

✳ For a neat appearance, work cross stitches with the top diagonals facing in the same direction.

✳ Thread up lengths of several colours of stranded cotton (floss) into needles, and arrange these at the side of your work by shade code or by chart key reference.

✳ Work the designs from the centre outwards, or split them into workable sections such as quarters. On larger designs, first work the main subject and then complete the background and any surrounding motifs or design areas.

✳ When taking threads across the back of a design, weave the thread through the back of existing stitches to avoid any ugly lines showing through on the right side.

✳ Use short lengths of thread, about 30cm (12in), to reduce the likelihood of knotting and tangling.

✳ Check your work constantly against the chart to avoid making counting mistakes and thus having to unpick your work.

✳ For smooth embroidery without lumps, avoid using knots at the back, and cut off excess threads as short as possible.

✳ Keep your work clean between stitching sessions by packing it away in its own clean plastic bag to prevent any accidents.

ACKNOWLEDGMENTS

Thank you to my husband Ian, for his help and patient understanding while I worked on yet another book. Thanks to my friend John at Outpost Trading for his framing skills and his smile when I appear at his door with my embroideries. A big thank you to Cara Ackerman and DMC for their continuing support. Thank you to John at Needle Needs for the wonderful 'Necessaire'. A big thank you to Wendy Butt, who found me some fabulous references when I needed them.

Thanks also to the following people without whose support my books would never be produced. Doreen Montgomery, for her guidance and support. Cheryl Brown for giving me yet another wonderful area of the world to create a book around. Linda Clements, whose skill at perfecting my text is invaluable to me. To Charly Bailey for the gorgeous book design and Karl Adamson and Kim Sayer for the fabulous photography.

SUPPLIERS

For information about products, catalogues, price lists or local stockists, contact suppliers direct by post, phone or email. Remember to always include a stamped, self-addressed envelope. If contacting them by phone, they will be able to tell you if there is any charge for the catalogue or price lists.

UK

Coats Crafts UK
PO Box 22, Lingfield Estate, McMullen Road, Darlington, Co. Durham DL1 1YQ
Tel: 01325 394200 (consumer helpline)
For a wide range of needlework supplies, including Anchor threads

Craft Creations
Ingersoll House, Delamare Road, Cheshunt, Hertfordshire EN8 9HD
Tel: 01992 781900
Email: enquiries@craftcreations.com
www.craftcreations.com
For card blanks and accessories

DMC Creative World
1st Floor Compass Building, Feldspar Close, Enderby, Leics LE19 4SD
Tel: 0116 275 4000
Fax: 0116 275 4020
www.dmccreative.co.uk
For embroidery fabrics, stranded cottons, metallic threads, Light Effects threads and other embroidery supplies and also Jayne Netley Mayhew cross stitch kits

Framecraft Miniatures Ltd
Unit 3, Isis House, Lindon Road, Brownhills, West Midlands WS8 7BW
Tel/fax (UK): 01543 360842
Tel (international): 44 1543 453154
Email: sales@framecraft.com
www.framecraft.com
For a wide range of ready-made items for embroidery, including card mounts

Impress Cards & Craft Materials
Slough Farm, Westhall, Suffolk IP19 8RN
Tel: 01986 781422
Email: sales@impresscards.co.uk
www.impresscards.com
For card blanks and craft materials

Needle Needs
1 Stockwood Farm, Pylle, Shepton Mallet, Somerset BA4 6TA
Tel: +44(0) 1749 830345
Email: needleneeds@ukonline.co.uk
www.needleneeds.co.uk
For the ultimate needlework station, frames and lights

> **For further information about Jayne and her work visit:**
> www.netzfineart.com/jaynenetley.html
> www.jaynenetleymayhew.com
> or contact Jayne at:
> jaynenetleymayhew@btinternet.com

USA

Charles Craft Inc
PO Box 1049, Laurenburg, NC 28353
Tel: 910 844 3521
Email: ccraft@carolina.net
www.charlescraft.com
For fabrics and pre-finished items

The DMC Corporation
South Hackensack Ave, Port Kearny, Building 10A, South Kearny, NJ 07032-4688
www.dmc-usa.com
For DMC threads and fabrics

Janlynn Corporation
2070 Westover Road, Chicopee, MA 01022
www.janlynn.com
For Jayne Netley Mayhew cross stitch kits

Mill Hill, a division of Wichelt Imports Inc
N162 Hwy 35, Stoddard, WI 54658
Tel: 608 788 4600
Email: millhill@millhill.com
www.millhill.com
For Mill Hill beads and a US source for Framecraft products

Zweigart/Joan Toggit Ltd
262 Old Brunswick Road, Suite E, Piscataway, NJ 08854-3756
Tel: 732 562 8888
Email: info@zweigart,com
www.zweigart.com

ABOUT THE AUTHOR

Jayne Netley Mayhew is a renowned wildlife artist and cross stitch designer. She takes her inspiration from nature and her designs are detailed and varied, from eagles and dolphins to lions and zebras. Her work features regularly in needlecraft and needlework magazines and is also available from Janlynn Kits and DMC. Jayne has written numerous books for David & Charles, including *Jayne Netley Mayhew's Cross Stitch Safari*.

INDEX